I0176760

The Pauline Ministry in

the Kentucky Mountains

Or:

A Brief Account of the Kentucky Mt.

Holiness Association

by

Rev. Lela G. McConnell, L.H.D.

First Fruits Press
Wilmore, Kentucky
c2015

The Pauline Ministry in the Kentucky Mountains, or, A brief Account of the Kentucky Mt. Holiness Association / by Lela G. McConnell
First Fruits Press, ©2015

ISBN: 9781621712039 (print), 9781621712046 (digital), 9781621712053 (kindle)

Digital version at
http://place.asburyseminary.edu/firstfruitsheritagematerial/98/

First Fruits Press is a digital imprint of the Asbury Theological Seminary, B.L. Fisher Library. Asbury Theological Seminary is the legal owner of the material previously published by the Pentecostal Publishing Co. and reserves the right to release new editions of this material as well as new material produced by Asbury Theological Seminary. Its publications are available for noncommercial and educational uses, such as research, teaching and private study. First Fruits Press has licensed the digital version of this work under the Creative Commons Attribution Noncommercial 3.0 United States License. To view a copy of this license, visit http://creativecommons.org/licenses/by-nc/3.0/us/.

For all other uses, contact First Fruits Press

McConnell, Lela G. (Lela Grace), 1884-1970.
   The Pauline ministry in the Kentucky mountains, or, A brief account of the Kentucky Mt. Holiness Association / by Lela G. McConnell
   200 pages, viii, : illustrations, portraits ; 21 cm.
   Wilmore, Ky. : First Fruits Press, ©2015.
   Reprint. Previously published: Berne, IN : Economy Printing Concern, [195-?]. Ninth edition.
   ISBN: 9781621712039 (pbk)
   1. Kentucky Mountain Holiness Association -- History. 2. Missions -- Kentucky. I. Title. II. Brief account of the Kentucky Mt. Holiness Association.
BX7990.H62 K4 2015

Cover design by Wesley Wilcox

First Fruits Press
The Academic Open Press of Asbury Theological Seminary
204 N. Lexington Ave., Wilmore, KY 40390
859-858-2236
first.fruits@asburyseminary.edu
asbury.to/firstfruits

LELA G. McCONNEL
President and Founder
of the
Kentucky Mountain Holiness Association

THE PAULINE MINISTRY IN THE
KENTUCKY MOUNTAINS

The Pauline Ministry in the Kentucky Mountains

Or:

A Brief Account of the Kentucky Mt. Holiness Association

By Rev. Lela G. McConnell, L.H.D.

Ninth Edition

—

Printed by

ECONOMY PRINTING CONCERN, INC.
Berne, Indiana

[Printed in the United States of America.]

This book was originally published with picture plates dispersed throughout the text. In this current version, the pictures have been moved to the front. The Captions from the original publishing are provided. -First Fruits Press, 2015

Plate 1 - Printed between pages 42 & 43

Out station pastors of the Ky. Mt. Bible Inst.

Bottom—KMBI Choir on a tour to our many Pastorates.

Plate 2 - Printed between pages 106 & 107

Early Camp Meeting. Out station Church and Parsonage. Early Days Commencement at Mt. Carmel H. S.

iv

Plate 3 - Printed between pages 138 & 139

Mt. Carmel H. S. Campus 1941. June Conference 1942. KMBI Campus 1941.

Plate 4 - Printed between pages 194 & 195

Terrace Garden on Mt. Carmel Campus. Swinging Bridge Across the **Ky.**
River. Our First June Conference of the Workers.

INTRODUCTION

Rev. Lela G. McConnell has written a history of her marvelous work in the Kentucky Mountains which will be read with deepest interest by the ones who are fortunate enough to receive a copy.

The title of this book is "The Pauline Ministry in the Kentucky Mountains," and is most appropriate for the work that has been accomplished by this woman of dauntless courage and marvelous faith. I have often said that Rev. Lela G. McConnell has done more for the spiritual uplift of Kentucky in her ministries to our mountain people, than all the churches in the State.

She now has work reaching into seven counties with the message of full salvation; students from fourteen counties attend the Mt. Carmel High School and the Kentucky Mountain Bible Institute. She has ninety-eight sanctified men and women who teach, preach and help in her schools and churches.

If you want a book that reads like the Acts of the Apostles secure this book and marvel, with me, at the things which God has accomplished through this woman who "knows nothing save Jesus Christ, and Him crucified." Marvelous work! Marvelous woman! Marvelous reward! Marvelous Christ!

As a Kentuckian, I personally am grateful to Rev. Lela G. McConnell and her sacrificial assistants, for bringing to the mountain people of Kentucky the intellectual and spiritual training they would not otherwise have received, had she not heard the Master's call and heeded His promise, "The mountain shall be thine."

In grateful appreciation,

MRS. H. C. MORRISON.

DEDICATION

To the faithful pastors, teachers, and helpers of the Kentucky Mountain Holiness Association and to the Executive Committee, Mr. and Mrs. R. L. Swauger, Miss Martha Archer, Miss Genelle Day. Mrs. H. P. Myers, and Rev. Carl Faulkner, this book is prayerfully dedicated by the author.
March 21, 1942.

Lawson, Breathitt County, Kentucky.

FOREWORD

As I traveled over the country telling of God's workings through the Kentucky Mountain Holiness Association a number of my friends suggested that I write a book relative to the work.

I have endeavored, therefore, in this volume to give a rather complete history of our interdenominational work of faith in the Mountains of Eastern Kentucky.

The material has been taken from my diary and from my own remembrance of the various happenings and events.

Nothing can be more helpful to the faith of God's children than the evidence of His faithfulness in demonstrating His truth and power in the many answers to prayer found in this book.

No greater satisfaction could come to the author than to know that the true incidents and remarkable answers to prayer recorded here have blest and helped those who read this book.

I am greatly indebted to dear Mr. and Mrs. C. Kildow Lovejoy for giving me a room in their lovely hotel, "The Ritz," in Paducah, Kentucky, where I could rest and write. The Lord bless them good.

The prayers of the pastors, students, and teachers in our Kentucky Mountain Holiness Association in my behalf greatly helped as I wrote. I felt their lift in a remarkable way over the stretch of four hundred and twenty-five miles across the State of Kentucky from Lawson, Breathitt County, to Paducah.

LELA G. MCCONNELL.

CONTENTS

CHAPTER   PAGE

1. A Sketch of the Author's Life and Her
   Religious Experience   7

2. God's Call To The Mountains. 32

3. Early Days—Tremendous Conflicts 41

4. Pure and True Americans—Their Surround-
   ings. 68

5. Up Against The Inevitable 93

6. The Pauline Ministry 110

7. Remarkable Answers To Prayer 144

8. Helpful Advice To Christians—Especially To
   Christian Workers. 169

9. Progress And Summary.—Joshua 17:18 196

CHAPTER I

A Sketch of the Author's Life and Her Religious Experience

"What I do thou knowest not now, but thou shalt know hereafter." Jesus spoke these words to His disciples. Often in my life has this promise come to pass. Why did the Lord permit me to be born on a farm? Why did I have to work so hard? Why so poor? Why so few luxuries? Why did I have to rustle for an education? Why so much prevenient grace thrown around me from early childhood? To lay a good foundation for a rugged ministry in the Mountains of Eastern Kentucky.

My precious Mother, who was named Rebekah Martha Elizabeth Eshelman, after her mother and her two grandmothers, was saved early in life at a Methodist altar. She gave me a good start even before I was born into this world. I am the youngest of seven children. She told me how the Lord came upon her in a marked way all during my prenatal days. She read the Bible and prayed and sang and rejoiced in the Lord as never before.

No doubt this largely accounts for my deep heart hunger after God as far back as I can remember. In early childhood I would pray in the attic, in the barn, and in my room alone. Visitors often remarked about my bent after spiritual things and thought it was very remarkable.

Sometimes Mother would get blest and walk up and

down the aisle of the church waving her hand in the air. Her face was filled with the glory of God. I would cry and want to love Jesus too.

In 1895, Brother McComas, the pastor of the Methodist Church in Honey Brook, Pa., was holding a revival meeting in the country school-house called Poplar Grove. This was just one-half mile from our home. Father got under deep conviction and raised his hand for prayer. Mother shouted. I can see her yet. God used it to bring great conviction on the unsaved. Father did not like it. The devil was stirred. After we reached home, father shook his fist in mother's face and said, "Beckie if you shout again, I'll never go to the altar." A few weeks later a revival began in the church in Honey Brook. This was one mile from our farm. Conviction fell on the people. Many came to the altar. Frequently they would spend days seeking the Lord. "Did he get through?" "Did she get through?" were questions one could often hear in those days. Folk kept on seeking until they found God. They confessed their sins and plead with God for mercy. One man was deeply convicted for his sins and God was mightily dealing with him. The preacher asked him to come to the altar. He became very angry and left the church in a rage. Others ran to the altar crying for God to save them. These gracious scenes made an indelible impression on my mind and heart. It was in this meeting that father was again moved upon. He fell at the altar and sought the Lord desperately for a few nights. The burden became so heavy one afternoon that he came into the house from the woodpile, where he was cutting wood, and said to mother, "Let's pray." Mother prayed; then father prayed. While mother was praying the second time, he jumped up and said, "I've got it, I've got it." He shouted all over the downstairs of our big farm house. The neighbors, we children, and the cattle all knew that Henry McConnell had religion. I can hear him singing yet, "Oh happy day when Jesus washed my sins away."

People talked about salvation on the streets and in their homes. As a result of that one revival there were scores of heads of families and many young people who joined the church. One of the outstanding converts was a fearful drunkard who had a large family. The powerful change in his life and home brought much glory to Jesus. His testimony was filled with great love to God for saving him from drink. Many times I missed Sunday school and went into the class meeting just to hear father and mother and others testify. The leader, Jessie Layton, would lead in some appropriate grand old song after nearly every testimony. He would exhort with blessing and thus encourage the saints to press on.

In the great Love Feast seasons, which were held on Sunday morning once a month, the people of God had great liberty in praising the Lord and in telling of His blessings and goodness to them. The house was filled and there was seldom enough time for all of them to testify. Oh, the precious memories of those days of God's manifest power.

Father was mighty in prayer. In January, 1902,

when the revival was pulling hard, the pastor called on him to pray. God used that prayer to lift the entire service and to break the power of the devil. The people talked about it much. We were not able to go in the carriage that night because the roads were too icy. It was a very cold, clear, moonlight night. The blessing of God was so upon father that we hardly spoke a word all the way home from the service. That was the last time he attended church. At his funeral the preacher spoke about the wonderful prayer that father made that night in the revival. "The effectual fervent prayer of a righteous man availeth much." Jas. 5:16.

In February, in his fifty-second year, he became very ill. The doctor, who was my uncle, told mother that he could not get well. The preacher came and asked mother what he could do. She said, "Pray that Henry will regain consciousness so that we may have one more testimony of his safe home-going." At 4:00 P. M., on the 16th of February he raised up in bed and sang so clearly, "I want to go there, I want to go there." All of us children and mother stood around the bed and cried. The glory of God filled the room. He talked about Jesus and Heaven through the night. The next morning at 7:00 o'clock, his spirit went sweeping through the gates washed in the Blood of the Lamb.

I firmly believe that the Lord sanctified father fifteen hours before he died. Many true Christians, who have never had the light on full salvation, are thus made clean on their death bed. Some who are so victorious and who eagerly walk in all the light they have, I believe, have received the blessing some time along in their life and did not know what to call it. I have heard some of them say the first time they hear it preached, "Why, I received that experience back there," and they relate very clearly just how and when it happened. Others say, "Well, my father and mother or some relative died very happy and they lived a true Christian life and yet never were sanctified, and I know they went to Heaven." God has seen them and knows them through and through, and He either sanctified them on their death bed or sometime in their lives or they could not have gone to Heaven. If folk have backed down on light and fought holiness, it's a different story. God is faithful to all who truly love and obey Him. He will sanctify them just as He takes care of the cleansing of the Adamic nature or carnality in children who die under the age of accountability, for all are born with this nature in them. Praise God for the provision made on Calvary for the taking out of "inbred sin" and thus preparing us to go to heaven where no sin can enter. Psalm 24:3, 4, "Who shall ascend into the hill of the Lord, or who shall stand in his holy place? He that hath clean hands, and a pure heart." Matthew 5:8, "Blessed are the pure in heart; for they shall see God." Hebrews 12:14, "Follow peace with all men, and holiness, without which no man shall see the Lord."

I knew of a case in Bristol, Pa. A dear Presbyterian lady, who had lived a good and consistent Christian life, came down to her death bed. Her granddaughter told us how fearful she was of death and the judgment. She cried and prayed unto the Lord. Finally, she sent for her pastor. He failed to help her. She called for another preacher in town. Not any of them were able to give her the light she needed. She prayed on. One day the Lord came with great joy and victory to her heart. After that she lived a number of weeks, but with no fear of death or the judgment. Carnality had gone. Her soul was restful and quiet in the joy of this new victory. Her granddaughter and others told me that they could not understand it. I told them I knew perfectly what had happened; the Holy Ghost had come into her heart in sanctifying power. Matthew 5:6, "Blessed are they which do hunger and thirst after righteousness: for they shall be filled."

The Lord, through the family altar and the rich grace of God upon father and mother, kept deepening the conviction that had been on my heart ever since my very earliest recollections.

When I was thirteen years old, another revival was held in our Methodist Church in Honey Brook in January. Miss Amy V. Plank, now Mrs. Dr. Hoffman, who had been my school teacher, came and spoke to me. She said, "Lela, wouldn't you like to be a Christian?" I began to cry and she led me to the altar, and there I confessed my sins and prayed for the Lord to forgive me. One fearful lie I had told come before me. It had bothered me much. I made it right with mother and my sister Mabel. I had borrowed her skates. She wanted to take them to High School the next day.

I said I had given them to one of the boys to sharpen and that I would get them for her tomorrow. The truth of the matter was, I had hidden them under the fence on my way home from school and planned to use them the next day to go skating on Griffith's Pond near the Poplar Grove schoolhouse. After seeking for some time, the Lord so sweetly met my soul and forgave all my sins. I was happy in Him. The fear of dropping into Hell during a thunder storm was gone. I would go to sleep at night knowing that the prayer I had repeated every night through my childhood would be true: "Now I lay me down to sleep, I pray Thee, Lord, my soul to keep. If I should die before I wake, I pray Thee, Lord, my soul to take." I now sang from my heart with father and mother, "Oh happy day, when Jesus washed my sins away."

The pastor, W. Q. Bennett, assigned me to the Tuesday night Class Meeting when I joined the church. I often walked alone in the dark to attend these meetings because I loved this service better than any other one in the church. I could hardly wait until the next service. Truly the words of the Psalmist were mine, "As the hart panteth after the waterbrooks, so panteth my soul after Thee, O God."

Often I visited the families living at the other end of our farm where the town people had built a reservoir. They had bought our big spring and some land around it to make a good sized reservoir for their water supply. This spring is the head of the Brandywine Creek of Revolutionary fame. I prayed and talked salvation in their homes. One man whose name was Alex

Story tried to argue with me many times, but when I prayed he would cry and ask me to come back again. The pastor soon began to call on me to lead in prayer in the public meetings. These things gave me courage and helped me to grow in grace, bear the cross, and keep blest. The enemy was after me persistently and tried hard to discourage me in my zeal for the Lord. I joined the Bible Study Class every winter and never missed a meeting. Many times I had to go alone when my sisters could not go with me. I was allowed to take old Nell, our family horse, and the buggy. I would come home about nine o'clock each time and put the horse and buggy away all alone in the dark. God was building into me some good timber for the Hills of Kentucky. "What I do thou knowest not now, but thou shalt know hereafter," says Jesus.

The four boys were the oldest in our family and the three girls the youngest. After the boys left home to work, it fell to my lot to work with the horses on the farm. To roll or harrow a ten-acre field was no small job for a thirteen-year-old girl. Sometimes the roller would come apart or the spring-tooth harrow would catch on a stump or on a rock. I would pray and the Lord would dry my tears and help me. The most trying thing was to load the hay. Often I prayed in the fence corners or on a heap of hay. I rode a horse without saddle or bridle with no fear. The creamery where we took our milk and that of grandfather's was six miles round trip across the country to Uncle George Emery's place in Cambridge. In warm weather I let the horse have her own gait, while I lay on the seat of

the big spring wagon and prayed most of the way
there and back. The men at the creamery were very
kind. They lifted the heavy cans of milk out of the
wagon for me. These irksome toils on the farm taught
me many valuable lessons for my future ministry
among the dear mountain people.

Revival meetings within four or five miles from
home, I often attended. I would hitch the horse to the
buggy or sleigh and get Bessie and Mabel, my sisters,
and away we would go over snow or ice, smooth or
rough roads. I would help around the altar, work in
the congregation, inviting sinners to the altar, and
pray and testify in the meetings. My love for the Lord
and for souls grew richer all the time. One night when
the roads were very icy after a light snow, we went to
Morgantown Methodist Church to a revival. There
was a steep hill over a mile long which we had to cross
and it was like a sheet of ice that night. I was not a
bit afraid because my trust was in the Lord In fact
I was fearless about a lot of things. The horse would
slip. The girls cried out and begged me to stop because they were sure the horse would fall down and
upset the sleigh, but God took care of us. We got there
and back safely and enjoyed the service. God rewarded us for our efforts. All of these spiritual exercises
were weaving into me courage and faith to help keep
me from ever backsliding or falling from grace in the
least. Those were good days to my soul. They help
me now to tell others the way to establishment in
grace. The church folk and the preachers were very
kind to me. They encouraged me in many ways. My

entire ambition was to live whole-heartedly for Jesus.

Central High School in Honey Brook Township was established a few years before I was converted. It was built largely through the efforts of my mother and a few others. Mother would walk for miles day after day, when father could not spare one of the horses, to get signers on a petition for the project. The subject was much discussed in our home. Nothing discouraged mother because the need was so urgent. The school was built. My two sisters were among the first to enroll. Hundreds of young people from the country were enabled to get four years of good high school training here. The school was two miles from home. I never missed a day except when my father died. Sometimes the students would say unkind things to me because I would not go their way. The Lord kept me. I really pitied them because they were so sad and discouraged with life on account of their sins. I would go to the church services and this filled my whole horizon; worldly things did not attract me. The Bible says, "If any man love the world, the love of the Father is not in him." God's divine blessings were in my soul sublimating all earthly desires and wishes.

At the age of seventeen I finished high school and the next year began teaching in a Quaker community in Chester County. Mother, having attended the West Chester State Normal School and having taught five years, instructed my sisters and me how to keep order in the schoolroom. There were many colored families living in this section. They worked on the farms of the well-to-do Quakers. About one-half of my pupils

were colored children. One large colored boy named
Norman Burton became quite a problem. I said to him
very firmly one day, "Norman, I'll have to whip you
good if you don't stop disturbing the school." Later
in the day he began to misbehave. I sent one of the
boys out to get a switch. I surely did give him a good
flogging, even though he was much bigger than I was.
To my sorrow, I got very angry. The boy needed the
punishment and it settled him ever afterward, but I
went to my boarding-house that day with a sad heart
I wept before the Lord and asked Him to forgive me
for getting angry and He blest me right then and there
I said, "Oh God, is this the best you can do for me?"

That winter I visited a very dear friend of mine
over the week-end. She lived in Coatesville, Pa. One
night we attended the Salvation Army. The meeting
was full of blessing. I know now that it was a holiness meeting. I said to her, "I'm going to the altar."
She said, "No, you're not, you're all right." I was
hungry for full salvation—"the second blessing" prop-
erly so called by John Wesley.

In the late spring I was taking some work at the
Keystone Normal School. My heart was hungry for
more of God. As the years went on carnality began
to manifest itself more and more. I wrote to a dear
Methodist friend whom I had known all of my life.
She was then living in Reading, Pa. I asked her where
I could go to get more religion. She at once wrote me
about a camp meeting at Delanco, N. J. The Teacher's
College closed just in time for me to go to the camp
for the full ten days. I went from the school at Kutz-

town to Philadelphia and up the Delaware River thirteen miles to the camp. This was my first long trip alone; but God was leading me and I knew He would see me through. The first service gave me enough light to know that I was saved, but needed to get rid of carnality. All the workers at the camp were Methodists: Dr. G. W. Ridout, Brother Powers, Cassia Smith, Clara Boyd, and Mr. and Mrs. Crammer. I went to the altar in the first service. I was an earnest seeker. No one had to coax me to pray out loud. I did everything they asked me to do. I was hungry for "The Blessing." This was what I was longing for almost ever since the Lord had saved me. Sometimes the workers would say, "I believe she has the blessing because she prays like it and acts like it." But I knew my heart was not yet satisfied. The camp had been going on eight days and I had sought in every service. The Lord was helping me to die out so thoroughly. Clara Boyd said to me, "Sister, put the unknown bundle on the altar." I said, "Yes, Lord." One day later I was sitting by a tent discouraged and tempted to leave the camp and go home. The devil was trying his best to defeat me. I was reading a little pamphlet called "Heaven or Hell, Which?" I cried unto the Lord and groaned in my spirit, "Oh God, I must have the blessing now." Instantly the Holy Ghost applied the Blood of Jesus to my carnal heart and cleansed it, and then He came in to abide. Sweet rest and assurance was mine. His glory filled my soul. The work was done and the Comforter, the Holy Ghost, had come. Rom. 6:22 and Gal. 2:20 were mine. I do not believe I ever had a wilderness experience because the first time I came up to Kadesh-Barnea I made a beeline for Canaan. Only those who back down when they come to this point, like the Israelites, ever wander in the wilderness. Since July, 1904, I have been living in Canaan.

The Word was made more real and blessed. I began at once to feed my mind and soul on holiness literature. Someone at the camp gave me "The Holiness Text Book" by John Thompson and E. I. D. Pepper, which is a book of holiness texts for every day in the year with a suggestive comment on each text. The texts are arranged and classified for a systematic study of Bible holiness under twenty different topical headings. I feasted on this little book year after year until I could repeat nearly every text in it. I would read the Bible contexts along with it. God revealed the glorious truth of full salvation to me more and more in His Word.

I subscribed for the *Christian Standard,* a weekly holiness paper. I would read every word of it even the advertisements. The Friday afternoon holiness meetings at 18th and Arch Streets in Philadelphia always had a page of their testimonies. These blest me much and helped me. This paper was a great means of establishment. It gave me the very light on holiness and the encouragement I needed early in the sanctified life.

In our home library I found "The Great Physician," by Phoebe and Walter Palmer. The strength and richness of this book lingers with me yet. One of my great aunts had Baxter's, "Saints Rest" and some of Wesley's sermons which I read with much profit. God will give us the desires of our hearts when our motives are pure.

The Life of Bishop William Taylor and the experience of holiness of Bishop Frank W. Warne, as related in the *Christian Advocate*, were a mighty source of help to me in the many trials I met with in my own home church. To my deep sorrow some of the dear people whom I loved and who had been so good and helpful to me before the Lord sanctified me, now made it hard for me. I could not understand it. Not twenty years old yet, and to have the preacher treat me so differently now, when before I was his "right hand man." The power of the Holy Ghost was so upon me that I could not keep from telling it and praying for others to get the blessing. I prayed much for the Lord to give me wisdom in my zeal for souls. God had so thoroughly planted the truth in my heart and head that He held me steady and firm.

I joined the Holiness Movement in the year the Lord sanctified me. Thus I kept in touch with camps and holiness conventions. This all gave me renewed strength from time to time. I began to realize that holiness was not popular, but that those who had the blessing were very happy and victorious. In the camps and conventions I found a host of the Methodists and others who were enjoying the same experience I had.

One dear old lady in our town said to me, "You think you have all the religion there is." This shocked me for I thought she was such a good Christian. Carnality surely can "act up" sometimes. This all kept me humble and prayerful. God never failed me; He

raised up true and tried friends for me. My only fear
was lest I grieve the Holy Ghost out of my heart. One
of my great aunts said to me, "I'd give the world to
have in my heart what you have." I prayed with her
and God marvelously blest us. Mother got hungry for
the blessing. I took her to Natilonal Park Camp Meeting in New Jersey. She went to the altar as soon as
she got there and the Lord met her in just a few minutes. The first thing she said to me was, "I had this
blessing once before and lost it." She enjoyed this
experience eleven years. One October morning in
1919, we found her lifeless little body in her bed. The
covers were not even disturbed—God had taken her
Home at the age of seventy while she was asleep. I
knelt beside her cold little form and asked the Lord
to help me take up the burden that she had laid down
—the salvation of the unsaved in our family. She always prayed for us children to find the Lord and not
be lost forever. God answered prayer. My sister
Mabel found the Lord in a revival at Coatesville, Pa.,
soon after mother's translation. This was three years
before her death. When my sister Bessie and I were
with her in the hospital in Lancaster, Pa., she was so
calm and patient during the two weeks there. The
nurse told us one afternoon that the doctor said she
would not live through the night. My sister and I were
on either side of the bed when I told her what the doctor said. At once she looked up and said, "Oh, that
will be glory for me—that will be glory for me, and
then I'll see mother." At daybreak the next morning
her spirit was wafted home to glory to be with Jesus

and to see mother and father. One more of the family housed safely forever in Heaven.

The Lord sent to our church a real and powerful full salvation preacher which greatly encouraged and helped me to get established in the sanctified life. He knew Greek and Hebrew as he knew English. He fed our hearts and God mightily used him to build up the church. All the finances were met without any money-making affairs in the church. He was untiring in his pastoral work and preached clearly the doctrines of the church. God bless the preacher who is a true shepherd of the flock. Jeremiah 50:6, "My people have been lost sheep; their shepherds have caused them to go astray. They have turned them away in the mountains." He fed the people on the living Word and built us up in the most holy faith. During all this time when the battles were long and hard, God was weaving into my Christian character the power of endurance. I was enabled to delight more and more in the power of the Old Rugged Cross. I was determined to make religion the every day business of my life and not a thing of fits and starts. I firmly believe that this is the reason why I was enabled to resist temptations and other things which get the best of many young Christians. While I suffered not a little ridicule and opposition from the firmness with which God helped me to stand for holiness; yet I rejoice today in the marvelous things which the Lord planted into my soul through it all. I can see now that God was preparing me for an unfaltering ministry in the hills of Kentucky.

After teaching four years in the country schools I

attended the Keystone State Normal School at Kutz-
town, Pa. I finished the work there in 1909. Here
many of the girls came to me for spiritual help. One
of them prayed through and was sanctified in my room.
The Superintendent of schools in Atlantic City, N. J.,
came to the Normal School for teachers. The principal, Dr. Rothermel, recommended some of us. The
superintendent interviewed the applicants and chose
four of us. I loved the city, the people, and the ocean
and worked hard at the teaching job. The superintendent gave me a life-time job under good behavior
with an increase of salary. I was then making more
money than any of my family. Here, in my fourth
year, God began very definitely to deal with me about
giving my whole·time to definite Christian work. I
settled it to fully mind the Lord. It was a happy day
in my life when I handed my resignation to the Superintendent, Dr. Boyer, in April, 1913. The Holy Ghost
flooded my soul with great joy and peace.

I was very active in the Central Methodist Church
of that city. I told the pastor about God's leadings. He
at once wrote to a Bible Training School in New England and secured a scholarship for me. In the meantime I met Mrs. Alda Beebe Prosser. She testified in
the Friday night class meeting about her call to India.
I had never seen her before. She had come to Atlantic
City for the summer to help nurse a very wealthy lady.
We visited together that first night until eleven o'clock.
I felt the pull toward the Chicago Evangelistic Institute when she told me about it. She had been a student
there for two years. It was a definite holiness school.

I gave up the scholarship to work my way through C. E. I. After I paid back the money I had borrowed for my two years of college work at the State College, I just had money enough left to pay my fare, which was $29.30, to Chicago.

The dear friends that God had given me felt led to send me money often. This strengthened my faith and taught me the very lessons I needed to learn about trusting the Lord for everything. Mrs. Jordan, Mrs. Eliza Eldridge, and the dear Central Church folk of Atlantic City will be rewarded much for their extreme goodness to me, also many dear friends in Honey Brook. God bless them each one. Many of them have gone home to Heaven. All who helped me have a good share in the souls that God has enabled me to win. The Loyalist Bible Class in Central Church had a farewell party for me. Miss Sadie Updegraff, the President of the class, presented me with a little red box which had many other smaller boxes in it. The last one contained a ten dollar gold piece. That was a great night. All of us parted in tears. These true friends have followed me through the years with their prayers and gifts.

Another farewell was held for me in Honey Brook. Mother wept and said she would gladly give me up for whatever field God would call me. The folk gave me some lovely things and some money. My heart was melted under the kindness of the dear home friends. Mrs. Ella Queen and others have stood by me through the years. Their share in the rewards will be large.

I reached C. E. I. in September, 1913. I shall never

cease to praise God for the years of training I received
at C. E. I. under Dr. Iva D. Vennard and her faithful
faculty. Miss Deborah Davis—so saintly and true,
Miss Susanna Swartz, so calm and deeply spiritual,
stand out vividly in my memory. They helped me
much. Also, Brother George Bennard, the author of
"The Old Rugged Cross," who was very efficient in
conducting the School Mission in the heart of the
down-town district of Chicago, was an inspiration to
me. I learned many valuable methods of Christian
work from him. Brother Joseph H. Smith came twice
a year and lectured to us on the deep things of the
Word and the Holiness Movement. Many times the
power of the Holy Ghost would fall on our chapel services and in our class-rooms. This training has followed me continually and has been invaluable in all of
my ministry. Here I committed Mrs. Vennard's,
"Heart Purity" book to memory.

The domestic work assigned me was ironing for
the faculty. The laundry was in the dark basement.
What a time I had getting victory over this. Then my
room was on the third floor with only one small window. I roomed with two young girls, one of whom
had no salvation. I had just left the "city by the sea"
which was very clean and the air invigorating. There
I had a large room alone on the eighth story of a fine
apartment house with plenty of good air and sunshine,
and where I could see the grand old ocean. The enemy
surely did tempt me about my present work and sur-
roundings in Chicago. All of this was good for me. I
never complained once, although at times I suffered

intensely in body in that dirty city. I was in God's will and the devil knew it. Thus he fiercely attacked me that first year. The Lord had already brought me through some hard tests which prepared me well for these battles. The good lessons of faith I learned by praying my way through C. E. I., are rich indeed now. In my senior year I felt very definitely led to spend all of my time studying rather than working to pay my bills. This was a mighty step of faith. It worked perfectly and gave me a splendid establishment in faith for temporal things. I left school with a debt of only fifteen dollars which I soon paid.

Three doors were open to me when I graduated from C. E. I. I went to Edmonton, Alberta, Can., where I helped to establish a Bible School and was elected the principal. Near the close of the second year my health failed. I stayed in the hospital for some time. A group of the students from the Bible School came to see me on Sunday morning. They sang, "God Will Take Care Of You." I took courage. God gave me the verse in Psalm 144:1, "Blessed be the Lord my strength, which teacheth my hands to war, and my fingers to fight." I knew then He yet had more work for me to do. With the temperature often fifty degrees below zero, I was compelled to leave the country. God gave me many true friends in Edmonton. A few years later Rev. Dauhm called me back to take charge of a mission in the city of Edmonton but I could not go.

The Lord so definitely healed my body that I was out of active Christian service for only nine weeks.

Dear Brother and Sister Shepherd of Gaines, Michigan, kept me in their lovely new home for a few weeks. God bless their memory. Their daughter, Blanche, had come to take my place in the Bible School before I left the Northwest. While skating on the ice one day in Edmonton, I talked to Clifford and Willard Hollman about their souls. This was the first time that anyone had spoken to them about getting saved, they said. From then on, God began to deal much with Clifford. Soon he yielded fully to the Lord. Both boys were attending business college in the city at that time. Today they are in full time service for the Lord singing and preaching full salvation.

Rev. John T. Hatfield, the Hoosier Evangelist, came to conduct a revival in the Beulah Mission in Edmonton. He was marvelous. My soul was blest under his searching messages. He was truly a man of God, a clear-cut, Holy Ghost filled preacher. He uncovered the sins of the people. The superintendent of the Mission was disturbed. I overheard her say, "If he keeps on preaching this way, he will have us all at the altar." Later I learned that she needed to be dug out. If only she had listened to the Spirit's dealings with her then—how different would have been her life. "Where one member of the body suffers they all suffer." A train of endless suffering has followed her and the work of holiness in that city ever since.

I left Gaines, Michigan, and came home to Honey Brook, Pa., to see mother and my friends for a few days. I then went to Atlantic City to rest for a little while with dear Mrs. Eliza Eldridge. The Central

Methodist Church pastor and board had a meeting immediately after the first Sunday I was there. They asked me to do pastor's assistant work for them. I accepted and felt so happy in the work. After a few years in this kind of work, I felt led to enter the evangelistic field where I could be free to preach and teach full salvation.

While in the pastor's assistant work, I helped Methodist pastors in Philadelphia and Bristol, Pa. Unless the preacher is a holiness man, it is very hard to get folk into the blessing of a clean heart. I made 1800 calls in six weeks while working for a pastor in Philadelphia. I said to myself, "Anyone—even a child seventeen years old, could do what I am doing and without any salvation." The pastor urged me to get the job done because he wanted the report for conference so that he could have some centenary funds to enlarge the church. I was not even allowed to take time to pray in the homes. However, often I did; and thus many dear people were helped and comforted. This was just after the first World War.

The Board of Church Extension gave me the choice of two other jobs after I had finished the one mentioned above. They explained the work to me and added that since it was in a foreign section of the city, I was to be very careful about telling the folk about Jesus. My heart sank with grief. I resigned and went immediately to holding revival meetings. In the very first meeting on the second Sunday morning, five women came to the altar seeking holiness. The pastor was so angry he would not even kneel when we prayed

with them. He said, "These are my best members."
However, God softened his heart as the meeting pro-
gressed and he asked me to hold another meeting at his
other appointment, which I did. The gracious liberty
and unction that the Holy Ghost gave me as I preached
His Word brought good results. Three different pastors sought the Lord to be sanctified in my meetings.
A pastor in Bangor, Pa., said to the people of the
church one night during the altar call, "If you will
come and seek what we have heard preached so clearly
from the Word tonight, I'll follow you." This same
man was my pastor when I came home from the camp
where the Lord sanctified me.

When we enjoy the blessing and preach messages
that revolve around the fact of a full, free, and present salvation; a salvation from all sin, its guilt, its
power and its inbeing; a salvation into the glorious
image of God obtainable by faith, we are bound to have
definite results and folk will be fully delivered from
sin and established in holiness. O, how great are the
privileges of believers! William Carvassa, the great
class leader of England, said, "As holiness is neglected, the work declines; as it is stressed, the work re-
vives."

The words of Jesus to His disciples in John 13:7,
"What I do thou knowest not now; but thou shalt know
hereafter," were again vindicated in my life.

After Mother died, I made my home with Mr. and
Mrs. Lewis Frame, of Chatham, Pa. They were exceedingly good to me. After my evangelistic meetings
they would meet me at the train or take me long dis-

tances over the country. Their prayers and help will never be forgotten. Also, for the dear Chatham friends, who still continue to help me, I am most grateful. The Lord is mindful of all of their share in helping me then and all through these years of soul winning.

I must relate two very interesting things that happened while doing pastor's assistant work. A dear saint of God asked me, with a few others of the church, to lead a meeting in her house for the promotion of holiness. I gladly consented. The meetings were well attended and the blessing of God was mightily upon them. Many folk were truly blest and helped, and some were definitely sanctified as a result of the services by getting hungry enough to attend a holiness camp meeting near by, and there the Lord sanctified them. The pastor, who was opposed to holiness reported the meeting to the Bishop in Philadelphia. He said I was trying to organize a church too near his church. He said the discipline forbade anyone holding meetings within a mile of another Methodist Church. This thought had never even entered our minds and was never mentioned in the services. I was a licensed local preacher in the M. E. Church. I was asked to appear before three preachers and the Bishop. I did so with no other thought but that they would take my license from me. The Bishop asked me to relate to him about the holiness meetings. I told him the best I could and how the Lord was using the services to help so many church members, and that unmistakably the Holy Ghost was upon the meetings. He said no more and dismissed the case. We went on with the holiness meeting for three years until I felt led to go to Kentucky and attend Asbury College. Many precious souls are now in glory as a result of those rich, full salvation meetings in Bristol, Pa.

In another city where I was assisting the pastor, I was asked by him to cut out so much of this "holiness business." The devil told me I would lose my job unless I obeyed orders. I was then in my second year in that place. I went to my room and prayed. The Lord assured me that He would take care of me. I resolved not to compromise or let down any. The Holy Ghost warmed my heart. That night I went to the mid-week prayer meeting which was always well attended. The pastor called on me to pray. The power of the Holy Ghost flooded my soul so that I was able to pray in such a way as to bring a mighty sweep of blessing on the service. People wept as the Lord came so near. The meeting closed and people came to me by the dozens and thanked me for the prayer. I said, "Give God all the praise." They did not know what was back of it all. In less than three months the preacher himself was seeking the blessing of holiness. He came up against the question of the Masonic Lodge. The Lord very plainly showed him what he must do. He refused to mind God. The Lord always takes care of every extenuating circumstance when we have the purpose to mind Him. When we put our whole wills on God's side, He will do the rest and we have nothing to fear. "A mighty fortress is our God, a bulwark never failing," says Luther

CHAPTER II
God's Call To The Mountains

"What I do thou knowest not now; but thou shalt know hereafter." Why did God put the urge upon me to go to Asbury College in Kentucky when He was blessing my ministry in the evangelistic field so richly? I could not understand it. My friends could not understand it, but God knew; He had been preparing me for this new chapter in my life which brought me in direct contact with the circumstances which led so soon to my life work in the hills of Eastern Kentucky.

God gives to everyone of His children, without exception, those things which are to them the educational advantages, so that He can improve them and that will best suit them for their own work. Thus, I firmly believe He led me to Asbury College. The enemy tried to defeat my going. In order to help myself through college, I not only held revival meetings, but also sold books that summer. Over a period of ten weeks I was able to clear $300 selling books. The President of the firm called me by long distance asking me to come to his office on Chestnut Street in Philadelphia. He said, "We will give you a private office in this building and $2,500 a year to begin with, if you will teach other folk how to sell this book." The book was the Standard Dictionary of Facts. I said immediately right out loud, "Satan, get thee behind me." Then I proceeded to tell the gentleman what God had called me to do. I have often thought that the man himself had missed

God's plan for his life because of the way he responded.

The settled peace and knowledge of God's will in my heart was indescribable when I landed in Wilmore, Ky. They enrolled me as a Junior although one of the professors said I no doubt could finish in one year. I had assembled all my previous credits before coming Students were asking me to join the various organizations. Among others I joined the Mountain Missionary Society. This was an organization founded by Claude Mingledorff in 1915. Its purpose, they said, was to take the Gospel to the mountains of Eastern Kentucky. Each Christmas vacation and sometimes during the summer, young men would spend time holding revival meetings in the mountains. There was something that attracted me much about this work. I never missed a meeting. The more I heard about the need, the more the burden came upon me for the needy people living far back in the hill country. I was elected secretary of the Society. God was preparing me more and more for what He wanted to reveal to me later. A very marked blessing fell on me as I prayed for the mountain work.

I had arranged to hold five revival meetings in Pennsylvania, Michigan, and Indiana the summer of 1923 at the close of my Junior year at Asbury. In the meantime a very urgent call came to me from the Free Methodist Mission in Breathitt County, Ky. They said there was no money in it and that I would face some hard things and perhaps not a few dangers. I could not get away from this appeal. It was a challenge that I needed. I had a $20 gold piece in my purse which

I had won in the Spring Oratorical Contest. I said this will see me through. I canceled three of the scheduled meetings and started for Eastern Kentucky to spend eight and one-half weeks in revival work there.

At once I fell in love with the work. The hungry-hearted people, the crowds that attended our revivals, the often cracking of pistols, the fine large families, and farming the steep hillsides gave me a tremendous love for the people. For the first three nights I preached with much liberty and blessing on full salvation. The missionaries said, "We feel that you are on the wrong track. No one here is ready for holiness. We must get the people saved first." I was new. I then went to preaching on sin and repentance. The meeting began to lose power and conviction. I said, "I must mind God and preach so that the dear people will know how God delivers from all sin." I did and the Holy Ghost honored it. This gave them courage from the Word to know how the Lord could fix them up. The break soon came. Souls fell at the altar. Twenty-three sought the Lord. Most of them were clear cases of conversion and over half of them were sanctified later in the revival. This was the first awakening in the history of this community even though other revivals had been held here in the mission.

This was a most blessed and remarkable initiation for me to the mountains. While many souls truly prayed through, the devil was powerfully stirred also. Some folk openly fought the meeting. I remember one night in particular when they rocked the building and fired off guns so that it was like a war outside.

Some stones came through the windows; some cracked the weather boards. My soul was blest and calm. There was a window back of the pulpit where I was preaching. I thought surely I'll get shot and go to Heaven at once. I never flinched. God gave me great courage. He was getting me ready fast right then and there to answer when He later called me so definitely to the hills. The sweet assurance of His care swept over me again and again during the many unusual experiences that first summer as I endeavored to plant holiness in the rural sections of Breathitt County.

Some of the scenes I shall never forget. One man with fourteen children was saved and was seeking to be sanctified. He said finally, "The Lord has shown me that I must go and make things right with my brother-in-law. I have not spoken to him for nine years." He walked twenty miles there and back, and coming directly into the Sunday service he started for the altar. God met him in a gracious way half way up the aisle. He preached and exhorted, and shouted all over the house, and shook hands with everyone. Among other things he said was, "Miss McConnell, they have called us 'Bloody Breathitt' but it's sin that has done it all." This was the first time I had ever heard that term "Bloody Breathitt." "Only through the power of the Gospel coming into hearts like this," I said, "will it ever be changed." The Lord used this victory to bring more conviction on others and to bless all the converts. Soon folks were shouting everywhere. It was a glorious day.

We visited much in the homes, had prayer, and talked salvation. A dear lady said to me one day, "Missionary, I'm a fearful woman. I cut the blood out of my children and beat upon my husband when he comes home drunk." I explained to her how Jesus came to take all of that out of her heart. He will help you to be sweet and kind. He can sanctify you and your ugly temper and hatred will be gone. She said, "I want it." She came to the service that night and began seeking God. I said, "Sister, you can't get what I told you about today. You must have your sins forgiven first." She was an earnest seeker and a very capable woman. While she was serving the dinner one day, the Lord came into her heart in forgiving power. She ran out into the yard and shouted for one-half an hour. She sought to be sanctified in the revival. To-day she is a real monument of grace and is enjoying freedom from all ill-will, bad tempers, and strife. This is the old-time religion and it works everywhere.

The missionaries gave me $8.50 for my eight and a half weeks of preaching and long journeys on horse back or walking, but my soul was fully repaid in every way. I hastened to hold the other two meetings, one in Indiana and one in Northern Michigan in Methodist churches. Here the offerings were excellent. This made it possible for me to go back to Asbury for my Senior year. The vindications of God's Word that summer in doing the exceeding, abundantly above all strengthened me for the battles that were ahead.

As chaplain of the Senior class, I would often ask the folk to pray for God to lay it on some of the Seniors to go to the mountains of Kentucky and give their lives to this very needy Home Field, which was less than one hundred miles east of Wilmore. Finally, one of them said to me, "Miss McConnell, we feel it's almost a joke for you to be making this request. We feel that God is calling you." I admitted that He had been talking to me about it. After a struggle of six weeks, I said, "Yes, Lord, I'll go." The power of God flooded my willing heart assuring me that I was His chosen vessel to help take the message of holiness to the precious people in the rural sections of the mountains. When I testified to it, God bore witness to the people in Asbury College that He was unmistakably calling me for this work, and leading me to give my life in full time service for Him in Eastern Kentucky. This was in February, 1924.

Immediately visions of churches and schools in the far back sections of the mountains came before me. I could not sleep for the joy of the Lord upon me. I said, "And this is what the Lord has been preparing me for all the years of my life."

I firmly believe to mind religion young will save us from a thousand snares. God enabled me to always keep in His will. I praise Him for grace at all times so that I never backslid. I suffered not a little ridicule and opposition because of the firmness with which I stood for the right in my high school days and in my public school teaching, but I was set to make a real business of religion. My soul was so happy that I really pitied the unsaved and the compromising church folk. The Lord had given me a bit of seasoning for the hard tasks ahead. If God had called me earlier in life I might not have stood up under the heavy burdens and responsibilities that I have had to face. Twice before, and once since God called me to the Mountains, He overruled and did not let me get married. While it seemed hard at the time, now I am very thankful I can be without family cares and give myself entirely to the work of spreading Scriptural holiness and to the help and care of the workers. At a time like this, one is rarely able to get the mind of the Lord themselves. God uses faithful friends to pray and advise; friends who know God and discern His leadings. When a group of sanctified people are tremendously burdened over some move of ours, we may be sure that God is not in it. However, many young people will not listen to God's voice through their friends. They go on and then suffer ever afterward themselves, and cause untold heartache for others and greatly hinder God's cause. These individuals are a burden to any work of God and are always in the way. Some of them are chronic seekers and never get settled. They have married the wrong party and thus are unequally yoked together. God's call upon their life had to be given up or denied.

I have met many such people all up and down the land. They have a sad story to tell. I heard one of our best known holiness evangelists say at Eaton Rapids camp meeting, that nine-tenths of the people whom God had called into definite Christian work, and who have failed God, have done so through their social life. He related the story of his own daughter who almost failed to answer God's call to India through falling in love with a splendid Christian young man, but who had no call to India. What if she had failed God and missed these twenty some years of gracious soul saving work in India? I believe it is a very rare thing for God to ask any woman to go through life alone. However, for the Gospel's sake, He has required this separation of some.

Those who have had little or no light on these things have had to take God's second best. While others who have had much light and have taken their own way regardless of the checks of the Spirit and the kindly advice of their true friends, will suffer much and perhaps be lost forever. Our very worst enemies are those who advise us wrongly, whether they do it ignorantly or from some other motive. Our truest friends are those who will brave the storm and take the criticism which invariably follows in such cases. The flesh gets in the way of the Spirit so that they feel they are getting blest, when it is only the stir of their emotions and thus the devil has a good chance to deceive them. Gal. 6:6-10.

On June the first, 1924, Dr. Henry Clay Morrison, then President of Asbury College, handed me my diploma and said, "I give this diploma to the General of the Kentucky Mountains." I have found out many times since, that it takes a militant leadership. God's promises to Joshua, "As I was with Moses, so I will be with thee; I will not fail thee, nor forsake thee" and "Have not I commanded thee? Be strong and of a good courage; be not afraid, neither be thou dismayed; for the

Lord thy God is with thee whithersoever thou goest," have been quickened to me continually through these eighteen years among a pure American people hidden away in the recesses of the mountains. I have never doubted or regretted this call upon my life.

From this time on, I became God's handmaiden for a definite work. "Go in this thy might, have not I sent thee?" God said to Gideon and to me also. We speak of this one and that one as the founder of some work, but only as the servant of Him who is the founder of all. "He that built all things is God." Like Abraham, when God called, I obeyed and went forth by faith to be a sojourner in the Kentucky Mountains. As I look back over these eighteen years of the work with all of its failings on the human side, I realize that the Kentucky Mountain Holiness Association is a work of God. It is God's own building. There is no other explanation of its origin, its growth, its remarkable experience and its continuance. Yes, beloved, it was God who called me; it was God who trained me in the school of faith; it was God who ordained that I should found the Kentucky Mountain Holiness Association to help evangelize the extreme isolated parts of the Kentucky Mountains. Fully trusting in the sure promises of the Almighty, immutable God, I went forth. The records of these many years bear witness that there hath not failed one word of His promises.

CHAPTER III

Early Days—Tremendous Conflicts

Faith is seldom if ever in its earliest stages unaccompanied by tremendous conflicts. Through pain and sorrow, God kept laying the foundation of this work in the Kentucky Mountains deep in the heart of its founder. Since she was to be the leader of an army of workers, she must learn as a pioneer, through suffering and hardships, how to inspire others.

On June 1, 1924, Mrs. R. L. Swauger who was then Miss Mary Vandiver, a student at Asbury College and also definitely called of God into the mountains in March, 1924, came with me to the mountains. Also nine others came, including faculty members and students of Asbury College. Among them were Daisy Dean Gray and Dr. Hildreth Cross. Dr. Z. T. Johnson, then a student—later President of Asbury College, took us from Wilmore to Nicholasville, Ky., in his truck and trailer. Here we boarded the L. & N. train for Breathitt County. A little later we were joined by Mrs. F. W. Noble, who was then Miss Irma Cook, also of Asbury College. Miss Elizabeth O'Conner, superintendent of the Free Methodist Mission at Oakdale, so kindly took us into her home where we made our headquarters.

We had been given a new Bilhorn portable organ by Mrs. Jennie Luce, of Wilmore. Dr. Robert Steward, Miss Minnie Carmichael, and Dr. F. H. Larabee, of Asbury College, had each given me $25. With this money I bought a horse, a bridle, and a saddle from Mr. Jim Miller on War Creek and named her Beauty.

41

She was the most sure-footed horse that I ever rode.
Mrs. Swauger was the organist; Mrs. F. W. Noble the
songleader, and I was the preacher. We went from
place to place holding revival meetings in little schoolhouses. The Lord signally honored our ministry with
many souls who were saved and sanctified. We loved
the people and they were very friendly to us. The
crowds would gather, long before the service began,
and fill the building. Often there were more people on
the outside than could get inside. The work was very
interesting and the country most fascinating. Up the
steep hillsides we climbed and over the long winding
trails and through the creek bed roads we traveled.
Beauty carried all the baggage and lots of other things,
together with the organ; while the organist, the songleader, and the preacher walked. The long distances
we walked between the schoolhouses in the hot sun
gave us plenty of experiences in mountain climbing
and in surmounting many difficulties.

We felt at once that God had here a great open-
hearted people who had been waiting long to hear His
truth. Yes, for six generations past they had been
passed by in the march of time both by the church and
the State. The gracious liberty in preaching and
around the altar, where men and women were praying
through, encouraged us to press on from place to place.
The last meeting of the summer of 1924 was held on
White Oak Creek in Breathitt County. Here we stayed
in the home of Mr. and Mrs. Tom Haddox. Many years
before this a Methodist preacher had come through
this section of the mountains. Through his ministry,

Mrs. J. G. Lawson and Mrs. Blanche Haddox had been
made hungry for salvation and later were truly converted while praying alone in their homes.   In the
White Oak meeting Mrs. Haddox heard for the first
time preaching on sanctification.   She found out that
the Lord had given her this experience.   She related
very clearly what the Lord had done for her some
years after she was forgiven of her sins.   She had
never known what to call it before.

After I had preached on full salvation one Sunday,
Mrs. Sam Noble came to the front clapping her hands
and saying, "If there is anything more I want it."
Later in the camp meeting her heart was made more
hungry for the second work of grace.   She said, "I'll
have it or die, and there will be nothing between my
soul and the Savior."   God powerfully met her before
she reached the altar.   Today these two dear women,
Mrs. Haddox and Mrs. Noble, are on our board of
trustees.   We counted it a glorious privilege to witness
and preach to the hungry-hearted people and to tell
them of the reality of God and the certainty of His
promises in every home and revival meeting.

During the first summer's work it became known
that we wanted to build a boarding school with a
church in connection with it.   Consequently, many of
the mountain people in various sections offered us land,
lumber, and labor.   We prayed much about it.   After
several meetings on a little hilltop at the Lawson
graveyard on Mill Creek, where crowds would gather
to hear what the missionaries decision was about the
location, we felt very clearly that the Lord wanted us

to build on a far out-of-the-way spot in the extreme northwest section of Breathitt County, where the people had been deprived of church advantages and high school opportunities.

Mr. and Mrs. J. G. Lawson very kindly donated twelve acres of land on a delightful hilltop overlooking the North Fork of the Kentucky River and two miles west of the mouth of Frozen Creek. In August, 1924, the land was cleared and dedicated. We set a day to clear the land of small trees, sumac, and underbrush. Thirty-one people came to help. Many snakes ran from their hiding places. The work went on very well. Near the close of the day we had a marshmallow roast. Everyone enjoyed the day of hard work. I remember Mrs. Sam Noble and I setting fire to a very large pile of green brush which the men said would not burn. In less than an hour there was only a pile of red ashes.

Dr. F. H. Larabee and Mr. C. A. Lovejoy, of Asbury College, and many of the neighborhood folk were at the dedicatory service of the campus. The blessing of God was richly upon it that day and we have never doubted or regretted His leadings to this location.

It was during this time when we were having a season of prayer in the home of Mrs. Blanche Haddox that God gave us a name for our first church and school. Before we were off of our knees, Dr. Larabee said, "Miss McConnell, I have a name for your church and school. Call it Mt. Carmel." Thus God gave us the name. Every step of the work has been born and directed through prayer.

Mrs. Mary Vandiver Swauger left in September to go back to Asbury College. Mrs. Irma Cook Noble went to Huntington Park Bible School on the Pacific coast to teach. I was left alone in the mountains. I continued to hold revival meetings in the various sections and made my headquarters at Jackson, the county seat of Breathitt County.

The last of September I attended the annual conference of the Methodist Episcopal Church which was held at Maysville, Ky. On the train that morning my heart felt burdened over the great need of the mountains. The enemy tempted me sorely to discouragement. I felt so alone with no one to help me with the big task of holding revival meetings and the burden of the new church and school. As is my custom to read some portion of the Old Testament and some of the New Testament in my daily devotions, I turned to Joshua the seventeenth chapter. All the way through the Holy Ghost quickened it to my heart. When I came to the eighteenth verse, the joy of the Lord overwhelmed me. I dried my tears and gave praise to the Lord. This verse, Joshua 17:18, "But the mountain shall be thine; for it is a wood, and thou shalt cut it down: and the outgoings of it shall be thine: for thou shalt drive out the Cananites, though they have iron chariots, and though they be strong," has often been a mighty bulwark to my faith. At the conference Bishop Theodore Henderson ordained me a deacon. The examining board accepted my Chicago Evangelistic Institute and Asbury College credits so that I did not have to take the conference course of study.

I trusted the Lord for my every need and never took up an offering. I knew that nine-tenths of the people did not have any money to give. My faithful horse took me everywhere. In Jackson I rented a room for ten dollars per month from Mrs. Jessie Cundiff, who was a splendid Christian. She was very good to me. Here I made my headquarters for the winter. There was no church and no board back of me. I told no one my needs. The Lord let my faith be tested to the limit. Often I went to bed hungry. The house had water lying under it most of the winter. The devil said, "Now your kidney trouble will come back with all of this cold and dampness." My room was near the ground. I could not keep warm. During the extreme cold weather no revivals could be held in the little schoolhouses. I was in Jackson a good share of that first hard winter. Someone sent me an old canvas piano cover. It was truly a God-send. I put it between the thin mattress and the springs. I felt this was an answer to prayer. I told the Lord one night, "I'm here until I die; if I starve or if I freeze." God saw I meant business. Soon money came and I was able to pay for my room and get my meals at a restaurant. I attended the Methodist Church in Jackson and also a regular Thursday P. M. prayer meeting conducted by the good ladies of the town. These meetings helped me to get acquainted and gave me an outlet to my already overburdened heart. My soul fed on the Word through those long weary days and often I would pray by the hour until waves of glory flooded my soul.

Often during the winter I visited in the neighborhood of the school and church site praying with the people and discussing the plans for the buildings. Early in March, 1925, I advertised in the *Jackson Times* that a contract would be let for the foundation of the main building of the Mt. Carmel Church and School. On the day set Mrs. Sam Noble, Mrs. Blanche Haddox, Mr. J. G. Lawson, and others went with me to Judge Pollard's office where a number of men had gathered. Judge Pollard made out all of our legal papers. He said he wanted to have a share in the work. I would often go to him for advice about legal matters. He saved us many dollars and fortified us always against any future trouble with our deeds and other papers. Often we thank God yet for his help in those early trying days. After having prayer with the men and discussing the matter and hearing the different bids, etc., the contract was let for $1500, to be finished by May 1st, 1925. On March 10th while the people stood around, some of them weeping for joy, I dug the first shovel full of earth for the foundation. God's own seal of blessing was peculiarly there that day. I submitted the plans to the contractor. This large roll of blue prints I had secured in Irvin, Ky., from an architect for $100.00. We worked long and hard on the plans. Sometimes I would go to Wilmore to get some help about the plans. Finally, Dr. Larabee said to me, "We feel that you have the burden of it so upon you that we can trust you with it all." That was a big step for me. I know the Lord led in all of this because the plans worked out well and satisfactorily. The men finished the stone foundation for the main building on the date stated and received their $1500 in full. God had sent the money in direct answer to prayer. The first money given to me for the new church and school was fifty cents from a dear little mountain girl. It touched my heart when I learned that she had worked long and hard to earn the fifty cents by picking coal that had fallen from the freight cars as they puffed up the mountain near her home.

In June of the same year seven young men from Asbury College came to erect the building. Mr. Raymond L. Swauger was chief carpenter and overseer. The others were Hugh Townley, Fred Martin, Henry Wheeler, Francis Baldwin, Eddie Linder, and Hayden Camp. These young men loved the work and were powerfully blest during the entire summer. They prayed and sang and held services in the little schoolhouse within three or four miles of the campus. They had come to Elkatawa on the train from Lexington, Ky., and there the Lawson boys met them with teams to haul their tents, bedding, tools, and eats. It was an entirely new experience for all of them. I have met these men from Asbury College at different times since, and they invariably tell me with deep gratitude how God used that summer to enrich their spiritual life and to give them a share in the work in its early days. The mountain folk from War Creek, Mill Creek, White Oak, Vancleve, Canyon Falls, and Glory Creek came to help.

The building was finished and dedicated September 8. 1925. Dr. H. C. Morrison and others from Asbury College and a host of local people attended the dedication which was held during our first camp meeting. The camp was held under a brush arbor at the foot of the present campus on the Kentucky River bank. The creeks were all dried up that summer so that cars could run over them. Even the Kentucky River was fordable by car. There were six cars on the Mt. Carmel campus that day. The little O. & K. Railroad ran a special train to Frozen Creek stop which was two miles from Mt. Careml campus. Mr. Swauger and his crew had built a temporary foot-bridge across the Kentucky River. A big barrel of ice water was made. Many walked long distances. The weather was very hot and dry. There were eleven students and teachers from Asbury helping in the stations and evangelistic work that summer. They were there with some of their converts. It was a great day. Dr. Morrison was met at Frozen Creek by a car. He was disappointed; he said that he wanted to ride over the mountain on a mule. Old Beauty, my faithful horse, and I brought the sack of dynamite through safely, to blast the big rocks out of the trail so that cars could come through.

School opened the following week with a fine enrollment of ambitious mountain young people, most of whom had had the eighth grade in the little rural schools for two or three years. Every room in the two dormitories was filled and there were many day students who walked two, three, and even four miles. A finer group of students could not be found anywhere. They were not used to dormitory rules. We had many hard discipline problems that first year. Three of the boys got drunk and broke up some of the furniture in their building. Those were the days of mighty soul travail. The Holy Ghost held us steady and patient, yet not allowing the devil to run things. God had sent us here and He stood by us so marvelously.

One dear boy who had been drinking and smoking since early childhood gave us much trouble. God got hold of him and saved him and cleaned him up. The boys who were slaves to cigarettes got through to God and were delivered from the habit. Many were the outstanding victories during the two revivals that year. We majored on full salvation. The Holy Ghost took charge of the services so that scores were sanctified wholly and some called to preach.

On one occasion a number of the students planned to attend a party about two miles from the school. We forbade them going. They said, "We are going." We told them that no one was going to hold them here, but that if they went, not one of them need come back. These parties meant dancing and drinking. We prayed and trusted God fully. Not one of them left the campus. The matron who was older than the rest of us, had to go to bed for three days over the strain of it all. We were fearless and thus God gave us powerful victories over the devil and all of his plans to defeat the school.

Miss Martha Archer, of Asbury College, taught the seventh and eighth grades. She was so afraid she would lose her salvation if she spoke with authority to the students. They became very unruly. One of them threatened her with a knife. I said, "Martha, you surely will backslide unless you handle these situations with a commanding voice." She did, and God used it to take care of the situation. A few bad boys can upset things, and especially when they think they are a law unto themselves, as the mountain young men were.

Crowds of men and women attended the regular night services and the revival services which were held twice every year. They came from far and near. One could hear the horses as they galloped by twos and threes, and sometimes more, over the trails. Almost all the young men carried one or two guns. While folk were praying through at the altar and shouts of victory filled the house, you could hear the guns crack and see the fire in every direction as the boys rode off through the night. The front terrace has hundreds of bullets in it.

The young men who were not students would want to make friends with some of the boarding school girls. This grieved us much, as well as the parents of the girls, who had sent them to us for an education. We worked hard to handle this problem. A boy with a gun and partly drunk can be very unreasonable. One of our day school girls came to me and told me of a plot of the outside boys. They had planned to shoot up the place that night. I said to her, "Oh, no they won't. We are here under divine appointment and this is God's place." We went to our knees in the office where the faculty had frequent prayer meetings. The Lord assured us He would take charge of the situation. The service began. The young men filed in by the dozens with their guns on their hips and moonshine whiskey on their breath. All was calm. God gave the preacher, Mr. Vincent, unusual liberty that night. The young men never knew what had happened or why they were restrained so that not one thing out of order occurred. God was there and took entire charge of the whole place. This was true over and over again during those early days of tremendous conflicts with the devil.

No wonder Miss Archer battled over a call that God was laying on her for this work. However, the encouragements far outweighed the conflicts. In December she settled it to spend her life for God and holiness in the Kentucky hills. She has been a mighty factor in the work ever since.

While all of the foregoing battles and victories were upon us, we also had many other difficult problems A $25,000 debt had to be met. The only solution I can give when people ask about the way we were able to get credit for so much and almost strangers in a strange land is, "God was in it and our faith never wavered." We simply stated our needs to the lumber company and other business firms in Jackson and they would let us have all we needed. We owed the Jackson Builders Supply Company $12,500, the plasterer $1,200, the men who did the hauling of the lumber from the railroad $1,100, the furnace $2,500, and many other bills. The running expenses also had to be met constantly.

We were almost unknown except through Asbury College. We never asked for money, but fully trusted the Lord. Asbury stood by us with a fine offering once a year. God bless Asbury College for giving us money and teachers through these years. The depression came on and they felt they could not help us as they had been doing. Our creditors were getting quite worried. One of them was in such distress that he threatened to sue us. We held on to God, sometimes fasting for days. I had read "The Life of George Muller" of Bristol, England—the great orphanage man of faith, and felt the Lord wanted us to use a similar plan. Money was coming to us in greater sums all the time and thus God kept us encouraged. As the money came we divided it among our creditors. I often went to see them and explained everything to them. This gave them a greater chance to see the working of the Lord and to know that He was truly with us. We were the talk of the country. Everyone was watching us. Folk knew in the town of Jackson every time a note came due. One time we fasted and prayed for ten days. Only twice during that time did I take a little milk and some crackers. God came so near to us. The entire campus was pervaded with the power of the Holy Ghost. I never shall forget it. We were praying for $1,800 to meet a note. The Lord did the exceeding abundantly above things. When the day came we had $2,700 in hand to pay the $1,800 note with. Many times the folk in the bank would say to us, "How do you do it?" We would tell them that it was the Lord. In four and one-half years we were able to clear the entire debt in direct answer to prayer and in the meantime keep our running expenses paid. "As I was with Moses, so I will be with thee; I will not fail thee, nor forsake thee," and "Fear thou not for I am with thee," and many other promises were vindicated in our behalf constantly.

Some of us agreed in prayer that God would handle a certain moonshiner. An officer soon came and raided the place. One of the men thought I had reported it. He threatened to shoot me. I said to myself, "If he does, I'll be in Heaven the next minute." I went to see him in his home and prayed with the family. They invited me to stay for supper. We have been good friends ever since.

As time wore on more young people found the Lord and the school soon became known far and wide through the students and their reports of the kind, yet firm hands on them. Sanctified teachers with warm hearts and well trained heads will turn out fine samples so that one needs rarely to advertise a school. Today we have nearly twice as many applying as we are able to accommodate and with double the capacity as at first. The school advertises itself. The Lord has certainly enabled us to produce a marvelous group of students who are a tremendous credit to the mountain country as teachers, business men, housewives and Christian workers.

We had proven to the people that we were their true friends and that we could not compromise or lower the standards either educationally, spiritually or ethically. Our students are often attracted to Mt. Carmel because of the lovely play ground with its tennis, basket ball, base ball, croquet and other games. Also they enjoy the extra curricular activities such as quartets for boys and for girls, chorus work, debates, literary society and other programs. This last year, 1941-'42, we have students from fourteen counties of

Eastern Kentucky. God sifts them out and sends the very ones that He knows will get in line for His call. We are not just running an "A grade" accredited High School; ours is a school where the young people who are hungry for the Lord may come and find Him and get established in the will of God during four years of their High School days.

At the end of the third year, holiness of heart and life was already being enjoyed by a host of our young people. The mountain preacher who opposed us was the subject of our prayers often. We feared his influence upon our students who were so beautifully sanctified. But when the young people became more firmly established, they were able to so pray and preach and live that they won that preacher and helped him to see the Light. One dear man who could not read, but knew Jesus, always brought a blessing when he tried to preach. Another one loved to have the missionaries come and read to him and explain the Bible. He loved Jesus so good.

We now have a whole host of our young people who are preaching all through the mountains. They are filled with the Holy Ghost and with a real call of God upon them, and have a burning passion for the lost.

The first World War had a great influence upon the mountains. The soldiers came back with more knowledge of the outside world. They wanted schools, roads, churches and all modern improvements. They are getting all of these fast, except the churches. Only as the missionaries reach the people in the rural sections are they reached. Our work through the schools is turn-

ing out many mountain young people who are evan-
gelizing their own native hills. "The mountains shall
be thine and the outgoings shall be thine" is our entire
ambition spiritually and only for the glory of God.

We contracted with two men to drill us a water well
on the Mt. Carmel campus at two dollars a foot. We
were to pay them in three months. The bill was
$142.00. It took them a number of weeks to drill it
with mule power. We had paid them all but $19.00 at
the end of the three months. About ten days later a
deputy sheriff appeared in the office with a summons
for Miss Lela G. McConnell. I had never been arrested
before and immediately I could see myself behind the
bars in the county jail. The deputy explained to me
that we owed the well drillers $19.00 on the water well.
Our mail comes over the mountain eight miles on mule
back from the train. I talked to the sheriff until the
mail came. There was no money in the mail and no
money in the bank. I left the sheriff and slipped away
to pray. My heart was broken with grief. The Lord
soon delivered my fears. Asbury College had sent
each of the teachers five dollars for Christmas: Royal
Baldwin, Nina Dixon, Bertha Bartlett (now Mrs.
George Warner), Martha Archer, also Mrs. Chas. R.
Vincent, stewardess and Rev. C. R. Vincent, general
supervisor of the grounds, and Mrs. Winfred Lester,
the matron. Each one contributed so that I had the
$19.00. The deputy said, "You owe me $2.50 more
for coming over here. We took up another collection
from our Christmas gift money and the man walked
off very happy with his $21.50.

The first commencement there were no High School graduates. Twelve graduated from the eighth grade. The chapel was crowded and the students of the entire school took part. It was like a revival meeting. I felt led near the close of the program to tell the folk what had happened about the well and how it grieved my heart so much. I said, "No, I did not once feel like burning that man's house, or poisoning any of his stock, or killing him, but that we would gladly let any of his eleven children come to Mt. Carmel School and that there was not the slightest revenge in my heart toward him. I said, "Friends the Lord has sanctified me wholly and taken out all the ill will, grudge, and strife and caused me to love people who do us wrong." I went on further to tell them from the Word about salvation and that the Lord had established and placed Mt. Carmel right here in their midst for that very purpose. Men and women were weeping all over the house. After the benediction three big men dressed in overalls rushed up to me and said, "Is the man here? Is the man here?" I was very thankful that he was not there.

In spite of all the battles, we moved forward with holy fire burning in our souls. This was reward enough. The divine call was upon us, and even though the task was a difficult one and our talents few and we were hidden back in the fastness of the mountains without fame or money, we loved the people and our job. We kept claiming the promise, "The mountain shall be thine." All of the people were very favorable toward the school with its "A grade" State accrediting, but there were many who opposed us when the Gospel of full salvation got hold of some of the young people. Their testimonies and lives were such a rebuke to sin. The devil was furious. One man said he would like to drive us out of the country at the point of a gun. Today he is one of our very best friends.

Early in the spring of 1926, Raymond L. Swauger came from Asbury College to take pictures for our first high school annual which we named "The Mountain Echo." During the few days that he was with us the Lord dealt with him about a call. While he was in prayer in room number eight of the boys' dormitory, the Lord came upon him with great assurance that He wanted him to burn out his life for the salvation of souls in this great needy home mission field. God had fitted him so well for the work. He had studied engineering and draftsmanship in Gettysburg, and in the University of Pennsylvania, and was now finishing his training in a holiness college. He had also worked in a bank for two years. His faithful ministry in teaching and in building churches, schools, bridges, etc., had been invaluable because it had been done through Holy Ghost wisdom and for the glory of God. He was the first man called into the work. Today we have a splendid group of men who are also just as definitely called and fitted for the work. One by one God has laid His hand upon men and women for life service in the work.

Mrs. Swauger said she felt so directly led to take a business course in Asbury in connection with her other studies. God was getting her ready to be the secretary of the work. The Lord has endowed her with much wisdom and talent in art and music, both vocal and instrumental, all of which has been a great asset to the Association along with her versatility and spiritual life.

Miss Martha Archer had a splendid background of experience in teaching and deep spiritual life so that the Lord made her a mighty factor in the early days of the work. Through these years in her preaching ministry, she has honored the Holy Ghost so that scores of souls have prayed through in the revivals which she has held in the mountains.

The fall of 1926 Miss Genelle Day came into the work by divine appointment also. She was with us for the summer as pastor on Morgue Creek. We prayed much at the camp meeting in August for God to send us one more experienced teacher for the coming school year, since Miss Bertha Bartlett was leaving for China, there to marry Mr. George Warner. Miss Day testified before the camp closed that the Lord had called her not only to teach, but to spend her life here. There was great rejoicing over it and God put His seal upon it. Her capability as a teacher has been a marked blessing, and her powers of discipline through close walking with God have been the means of getting many of the students well established in the Canaan Land experience.

Almost the first question our visitors ask us is, "Why did you build so far back in the hills and on the opposite side of the Kentucky River from the only outlet to a highway?" There was no highway in this section when we came into the mountains. Furthermore, God heard the prayers of Mrs. J. G. Lawson and others for the school to be located in this community. Mrs. Lawson said to me, "I'm the mother of fourteen children. I have ten living and the youngest is four years old. I have prayed for twenty-five years for God to give us a church and a school. I have often walked in our yard in the night praying for God to help us and send some one to bring us the Gospel." While these folk were praying God was preparing a little farmer girl back in Pennsylvania to answer their prayers. Mrs. Lawson lived to enjoy the answer to her prayers only one year. The following tribute was given to her in our 1927 "Mountain Echo." "Gone but not forgotten—Mrs. Cora Lawson was translated to her heavenly home, June 11, 1926, at the age of forty-eight. It fills our hearts with joy to know that one more saint has made the landing safely. She was the wife of J. G. Lawson who so kindly gave the twelve acre campus for Mt. Carmel Church and School. Mrs. Lawson testified a short time before her death that she felt Mt. Carmel stood as a memorial to her prayers, and that it was the fruitage of her heart's deepest desire. Mrs. Lawson's approach to the door of Heaven was serene and beautiful, a benediction to all who witnessed it. (She could easily see the campus from her sick bed and often her family would place her cot out in the yard where she could see it better). It was beautiful and fitting that her funeral should be the first to be conducted in the Mt. Carmel Chapel."

Not only did we have the local work of Mt. Carmel, but during the summer months the work was extended into other sections of the mountains. Little houses were given to us to live in by the generous hearted people. These were located near little rural schoolhouses. We furnished them very simply with cots, tables, small oil stoves, and a few cooking utensils and dishes. These were taken from the furnishings of Mt. Carmel. After each June Conference it was amusing to see the pastors, who had been appointed to the various stations, get together and plan their outfit and assemble their goods. We had the new pastors who had come on the train put their hand baggage in our little freight house at the mouth of Frozen Creek so that they would have that much less to carry through the boiling sun and often deep mud. These pastorates were carried on with much soul burden, responsibility, and care. Regularly organized Sunday schools and church services and mid-week prayer meetings and children's meetings and Bible Study classes and revival meetings were conducted. The pastors did much visiting, praying with the people, and talking salvation, as well as caring for the sick and dying. Each consecutive summer as we held meetings in the same places, we saw richer and more permanent results because the people were becoming indoctrinated more and more in the Gospel of full salvation.

The workers trusted God for all their needs. The people of the community often helped them with vegetables and milk. The average cost aside from these gifts was about $1.75 per week for each one. Two evangelistic teams held the revivals. In 1926 we had thirty-nine workers who came from nineteen states.

Students and teachers came to us from the various Holiness Colleges and Bible Schools over the nation to help in our out-station pastorates. At first we opened these preaching points only in the summer. In 1925 we had twelve of these stations. In 1926 we added two more. In 1927 we added three more, making seventeen. It was heart breaking to the pastors and to the people to close the Sunday school and church services and to leave the converts without a shepherd all through the winter months. We prayed for God to send us pastors who could stay all the year. In 1927-'28 we were able to keep nine stations open all through the winter. This was the beginning of our permanent station work. Our many consecrated pastors are full of sacrifice and devoted to the people; hence their marked success. In my visits to these outpoints I have been blest and greatly encouraged to press the battle farther back into the mountains.

When I would make a tour each spring through the country visiting the Colleges to make an appeal for workers, I would always try to state the case clearly about the nature of the work—no salary—many hardships and privations. I further stated that no one ought to come who had financial obligations to their school. However, one young woman who was just finishing her Junior year at Asbury College came to me crying and said, "I do feel very keenly that God wants me in the mountains this summer, but I owe the college $100.00 and do not even have any money for my fare." I tried to reason with her. We prayed together and the Holy Ghost blessed us so good. I said, "Margaret, you come on, and we will trust the Lord for your debt and for the summer." There were fifteen of us ready to leave after the commencement that day. Margaret was in the group with her baggage, having no money, but weeping for joy, knowing that the Lord was leading her. Finally, one lady who did not know her predicament, slipped a ten dollar bill into her hand as she said, "Good-by and God bless you." I saw Margaret through the crowd on the porch of the girl's dormitory. She looked at me with a big smile and nodded her head. I felt so blest for her sake for I had many times come through the same good test and victory even to the amount of $500.00 or $1,000.00 need that the Lord met in due time. Her ministry was very fruitful that summer at a station in the extreme northern part of Breathitt County. She went back to college very happy, having taken care of her share of the financial burden of the station and with $30.00 in her pocket, that was sent to her in direct answer to prayer. Soon after her enrollment for the Senior year, the business manager, Mr. C. A. Lovejoy, said, "I want to see you in my office, Miss Thompson. Someone has sent in $100.00 to be applied on a worthy student's bill. I have put it on your account." Again her faith was lifted. Miss Thompson spent seven years with us after she had finished her college work although she knew God had called her to Africa four years before. She sailed for the chosen field in March 1941, on the Egyptian steamship, the Zam Zam. This ship was bombed by a German Raider on April 17 in the South Atlantic. Her lifeboat sank. Holding on

to her Bible and her purse as she floated on the big
ocean, she sang, "Jesus Never Fails," with no fear of
death or the judgment. After some time she was
picked up by a German lifeboat and taken on board the
"Dresden." She finally reached New York in June,
1941. Not only in those early days did the Lord send
us such true and tried helpers, but all through these
many years He has led them to us in this work of faith.

For the fall revival of the second school year of
Mt. Carmel High School, we asked Brother L. O. Florence, a Methodist, of Wilmore, Ky., to be our evangelist. He, being a Kentuckian and so well sanctified, was
mightily used of the Lord. He had not been preaching
very long. He was saved in middle life, but felt he
must mind God and preach. This was his first revival.
The faculty and Christian students prayed and this
helped the evangelist and gave him the very support
he needed to encourage him to keep on answering the
call to preach. It was a very remarkable meeting. No
one was in the way of the Spirit's workings. Nearly
every unsaved student in the boarding department and
many of the day students found the Lord. Brother
Florence has held thirty-seven revivals for us in our
stations and schools since that time, and helped us in
three of our annual camp meetings. Many times have
we thanked God for Brother Florence's share in claiming the promise, "The mountain shall be thine." In
1934, Brother Florence wrote the following in one of
our annual folders: "It has been my privilege to labor
as an evangelist with the Kentucky Mountain Holiness
Association for a number of years. The first revival I

ever held after I was called to preach was at Mt. Carmel School. Since then I have held many meetings in the Kentucky Mountain Holiness Association field. I was called to go to Index Church and School one week before Christmas for a revival where Mr. and Mrs. Horace P. Myers were in charge. The Lord came on us in great power. He gave us twenty-one souls saved and seventeen sanctified. I came from there to the Kentucky Mountain Bible Institute at Vancleve where we saw the most complete dying out to self that we had ever seen before. When I left, there was not one soul that was not both saved and sanctified. I am in a revival now at Mt. Carmel School where we have experienced the joy of seeing every boarding student, who was not already a child of God, seek the Lord and find Him in saving grace. There are ten now seeking to be sanctified. We hope to see this entire big family over into Canaan Land before we leave." —L. O. Florence.

This good revival in our Index station is a monument to this day to our dear Brother Myers who lost his life in the flood of July 4, 1939. Nearly every convert is still holding true, carrying on the family altar and helping in the church with their good rich testimonies and prayers. Brother and Sister Myers had laid a good foundation for the revival.

Very heavy financial burdens tested our faith to the limit. The fall of 1926 found us living in the 46th Psalm, "God is our refuge and strength, a very present help in trouble. The Lord of hosts is with us; the God of Jacob is our refuge. Be still and know that I am

God." The enemy would come in like a flood, but the Lord would always lift up a standard against him. We were fitting up new permanent outstations, the food bills were larger, and the financial burdens were increasing. "Our immutable God never changes," I would often say to the faculty when we would meet in our regular faculty prayer meeting four times a week.

Bishop Henderson sent us twenty-five dollars with the final request that we put our work under the church. He promised to give me $100 per month salary and the church would pay our debts. He sent the District Superintendent to see us. I said, "Brother, will you send us sanctified pastors and teachers?" He was very humble about it and said they could not do it. I said, "I believe the Lord will send them and will see us through." God saw our full determination to major on holiness in heart and life first, last and always. The Holy Ghost was honored. Our debt of $25,000 was soon entirely cleared in direct answer to prayer. Our running expenses were then $300 per month, which were met also by faith in a mighty God whose treasury has so much unclaimed deposit in it always. Incidentally, the majority of our pastors and teachers are Methodists. Out of our ninety-two workers today, fifty-nine of them are Methodists. We have found through these eighteen years that a sanctified Methodist makes an excellent worker. Their background and ethics are so well rounded. I love the old Methodist Church. I am a true Methodist. When the Bishop ordained me an elder in 1926, the question was asked the nine candidates for ordination, "Do you have the blessing of Perfect Love or are you pressing on after it?" I said, partly under my breath, "Bishop, I already have it." A wave of glory swept over my soul and spilled over on some of the others. The men began to weep. Praise God for the doctrines of the old Methodist Church. It was at a camp meeting, where all the preachers and workers were Methodists, that the Lord sanctified me. However, our present staff of workers represent twenty denominations and all of them are excellent examples of the true faith of the old line churches. Our work is truly interdenominational and we love all the churches.

Nearly two hundred years ago John Wesley wrote: "Never deny, never conceal, never speak doubtfully of what God hath wrought; but declare it before the children of God with all plainness and simplicity."

Through these pioneer days we had some of the nearest approaches to God that any of us had ever experienced in our life time.

CHAPTER IV

Pure and True Americans—Their Surroundings

A lawyer in Magoffin County said to me in 1927. "There are five thousand children who have no high school advantages here, and this is one of the most thinly settled of our mountain counties."

A lawyer in Jackson told me in 1924 that one-fourth of the mountain children between the ages of seven and thirteen do not attend school simply because their parents don't care or because they do not have adequate clothing or money to buy their books. He said, "Their lot is constant toil."

I sent for a Rand McNally census book. The population of the mountain counties of Eastern Kentucky was then over seven hundred and fifty thousand. I counted very carefully the small towns with a population of three hundred and over, also the cities. Then I subtracted this number from the population. I found there were 500,662 people living in the isolated sections of the Kentucky Mountains.

This group of people can rightfully claim to be the purest of American stock because they are Anglo-Saxons. They and their ancestors have occupied these hills for nearly two centuries. They are quick, active, mentally alert people with deep emotions, which are easily stirred. This makes their hatreds intense and accounts for the feuds of early days. The rural population live on hillside farms, spread over hundreds of square miles, with only occasional roads and practically none of the modern conveniences. Our people are very patriotic. They love the flag and the country for which it stands. In 1917 and 1918 more soldiers volunteered from Breathitt County than from any other county in the United States in proportion to the population. Furthermore, more soldiers returned from the first World War to our county than to any other county in the United States. We have the World War banner.

In many sections today the state and federal government has worked much in the interest of the mountain people so that they now have many more roads, far better schools, with High Schools in nearly every county, and in some sections the Rural Electric Administration has come to light up the mountain homes. Sad to say, however, that the church has not caught the vision yet. Only as missionaries from the various denominations take up the work are the rural communities to be reached. There are comparatively few mission stations of any kind in all of Eastern Kentucky. Some whole counties have not one church for regular Sunday school or church services in the rural sections where the people can worship. This is our great burden.

There are thousands of creeks with all of their branches and hollows that are waiting yet for the full Gospel message.

The Methodist Centenary Survey revealed that two-thirds of all the preachers in the southland come from the Highlands. The hills produce orators. Where in American can this be duplicated? From one community alone as the result of three months of schooling each year and under most unfavorable conditions, the following record is revealed: Over a period of twenty years from this little school hidden away in the hills of "Beautiful Breathitt" there came forty-two noted men and women: four doctors, seven lawyers, six preachers, nineteen teachers, and six statesmen.

The following quotations from the lives of a few of our young people who have graduated from our schools (High School and Bible School) will give you a fine cross section of the country and these splendid, pure and true American folk who, having been hidden away in the mountains, have been given a chance. These young men and women are now serving as pastors, pastor's wives and evangelists in our work here in their own native hills.

THE TESTIMONY OF ONE OF OUR YOUNG MEN

"When I was thirteen years of age a very strange thing happened. Missionaries came to our community, and service (meetin') was announced to be at one of our neighbor's. My curiosity about got the best of me. I wanted to see what a missionary looked like. My mother, brother, cousin and I went. I was all eyes and ears during the service.

"That night preparation was made to fix up an old barn for the missionaries' home. Every day on my way to school I passed this barn, and how mean I felt, because those ladies were praying nearly every morning as I went by.

"An announcement was made that there was going to be a revival in a few weeks, and Miss Martha Archer was going to be the evangelist. I did not know what these terms meant, but I was determined to beg my parents to let me go and find out what an evangelist and a revival were.

"One night while the evangelist was preaching, my heart felt like a ton of brick. While I was standing during the altar call, my knees were bumping together. I stood it as long as I thought I could. Then I went to the altar, praying, 'Lord, have mercy on me.' That was all I knew. Miss Archer saw my predicament and began telling me what to pray.

"She said, 'Tell the Lord you will be His boy.' I said that after her. In a little while the burden lifted and I was 'a new creature in Christ Jesus.' At the age of fourteen I entered Mt. Carmel School. Ambitions, money, and friends were pulling me, but that call to preach which God gave me in Room No. 8 in the boys' dormitory caused me more trouble than all of them put together. I felt, 'Woe is me if I preach not,' and thought, 'Woe is me if I preach here in the mountains.' It looked like nakedness, starvation, and rotten eggs to me, for I had had rotten eggs thrown at me once for even sitting among the preachers.

"I had sought holiness and thought I had it, but these things helped me to see I did not have the experience. As the song writer expressed it: 'I was tired of living such a life of fear and dread. I was hungry for the blessing. My poor soul it must be fed.' I felt very keenly, 'When I would do good, evil was present with me.' Sometimes I felt as though there was no use trying, but there was my call, and that Scripture,

'God's callings are without repentance.' When I settled the sin question in my heart forever, this thought
came to me, 'God's callings are His enablings;' also
'As ye have therefore received Christ Jesus the Lord,
so walk ye in Him.' He came with power over sin,
when I was fully consecrated to Him, and by grace I
shall walk with Him in that manner.

"I praise Him for the four years of high school and
three years of Bible School training. He has given me
the privilege of getting into definite holiness schools in
the Kentucky Mountain Holiness Association, and I
am fully expecting to answer His call on my life to do
evangelistic work in my own hills and to help other
hungry-hearted boys and girls to get saved and sanctified and to mind God."

THE FOLLOWING IS THE TESTIMONY OF ONE OF OUR
MOUNTAIN GIRLS

"The doctrine that some were born to be saved and
others to be lost gripped my soul at the age of ten.
My heart was hungry for salvation, but I thought that
I was one who was born to be lost. For several years
this burden almost weighed me down.

"I had been to church only a very few times before
I was saved. Under Miss Lela G. McConnell's work,
missionaries were led by the Lord to our community.
I attended every service. Two weeks later a Spirit-
filled evangelist came for a revival. Conviction gripped
my heart. One day while my sister and I were stack-
ing oats I felt I could bear the burden no longer. After
driving the horse back for another load of oats we

knelt in the edge of the woods and each of us prayed more than one time that I would get saved. While placing the bundles on the half-finished stack, I determined to settle it then. Sister helped me pray and the Lord met my heart. I knew my sins were forgiven. The Lord showed me two confessions to make to sister, and I felt good doing it. I meant business with the Lord.

"During this revival I received light on holiness. I was determined to have the blessing, by God's grace. I sought to be sanctified several times, but one Sunday afternoon at the altar the Lord helped me really to die out to the Adamic nature. He thoroughly purged my heart and filled it with His Holy Spirit.

"I was ready for high school and began praying that the Lord would make a way for me to go. God answered prayer. I received a letter telling me to come to Mt. Carmel to school and they would help me pray in money for my needs. I joyfully accepted. The Lord marvelously answered prayer, and I graduated. When I left home my father said he would not help me at all. He was opposed to my going to a holiness school, and he has not helped me even so much as to buy a pencil. I do praise God for a praying mother whose faith and prayers have held me steady through many hard battles.

"During my sophomore year at Mt. Carmel High School, God definitely called me to be a missionary in the mountains of Kentucky. I shall never forget His presence and blessing upon our hearts that night. I did not understand what the future held for me then, but the glory of the Lord was flooding my soul. Of course, I do not yet understand the things in the future, but God has given many happy surprises in these nine years that I have known Him.

"I shall never forget God's blessing upon my soul as I went to my first appointment to an out-station for the summer. I was going to help an older worker. I packed my clothes in paper boxes, stuck an army cot under my arm, climbed on the train, and marched down the aisle getting blessed all over. People looked at me, my bed, and paper-box suitcases. I almost shouted aloud in their presence. I was now beginning to answer God's call on my heart. I felt that I had more joy than all of them together. After getting off the train, we walked four or five miles. The road was rough. The rain was pouring. Our load was very heavy. We were soon wet and muddy but finally reached our destination. I could hardly eat supper for joy. Our little home had two rooms, one made of logs, the other of planks. It had been papered with catalogue leaves, which at this time were tattered and brown.

"Each morning I walked up a very narrow hollow in the woods to have my devotions. Sometimes the neighbors could hear my secret prayers. I was inexperienced in preparing messages and I was conscious that the Lord would have to do it through me, yet I used the knowledge that I had. I did not know that a sermon should have a theme. I knew very little about a text, but the Lord blessed as I prayed. I would first pray that the Lord would reveal the main topic of the message to my heart. I would get desperate about it

and would not let go until it came. I would cry and
thank Him from the bottom of my heart, quickly write
it down, and then pray for the text. I would keep
holding on until the Lord would reveal a text to my
heart. Again I would get blessed and thank Him for
it and write it down. Giving God all the glory, I can
say that He gave the outline step by step. I asked Him
to help me really understand the Scriptures, to speak
through me, and to make me a blessing for His glory.
The Lord always answered, for this was a need, not
just a want. I knew He had promised to supply all our
needs.

"These last few years have been just as glorious,
but in a different way. I am now a student in the
Kentucky Mountain Bible Institute. Words cannot ex-
press my love to God and appreciation for the privilege
of attending these two holiness schools. By God's
grace I can say that He is broadening my vision, increasing my burden, and strengthening my faith for
glorious revivals in the mountains of Kentucky.

ANOTHER MOUNTAIN BOY WRITES:

"I was born on Devil's Creek in Wolfe County, Ky.,
and was brought up in a home where none of the family of fifteen were Christians. Early in life I got a
prejudice against being either a preacher or a doctor.
Furthermore, I got the idea that every man who became a Christian had to be a preacher. This thought
troubled my childish mind. One day my mother, finding out the idea that I had, told me that every Christian man did not have to preach. That surely did

bring lasting relief to my mind about that question.

"Not having the advantage of church and Sunday school on the Creek where I lived as a boy, I did not know much of God's great plan of salvation, but I had enough knowledge about the Word of God to know that I was a sinner and that if I died in that condition, eternal torment was my doom.

"I learned of Mt. Carmel High School, and I believe that the Lord led me there as much as anyone could expect Him to lead a sinner. I was hungry-hearted before I got there, and when I arrived I saw the students and faculty living for the Lord and enjoying it, and heard their testimonies and saw the glory of God radiating out of their faces. I soon began to seek the Lord. Before this time I had gloried in the fact that I had never made any profession of religion. Now my attitude was changed and I began to seek the Lord, even though I did not get saved during that semester. In the spring I went out with an eighth grade diploma, very happy for that, but with a hungry heart.

"During the summer vacation my mother was stricken down with inflammatory rheumatism. One night as I was helping to take care of her it looked as if she were going to die, and I promised the Lord that if He would spare my mother's life I would give Him my life. She lived through the night, and the next morning I went out in the woods alone to fulfill the vow which I had made to the Lord. As usual the devil was there to fight, and with the limited knowledge of a mountain boy as how to get saved, I went away without having prayed through. During the affliction of mother, my grandmother came to visit us, and while there she had prayer with us. One thing she said to me which made a lasting impression on my mind was a quotation from David to Solomon, 'Show thyself a man.' Grandmother told me later of her experience of getting sanctified in Campton, the county seat of Wolfe County, Ky. That was back in the days when they rode to church in an old jolt wagon. Folks would take the family and drive for miles to get to revivals. While attending a revival meeting she got the light on holiness through an Asbury College preacher and began to seek the blessing. When time came for them to go home, they got into the wagon and started towards Devil's Creek. As they went along, her faith took hold of God and the Holy Ghost came into her heart. She, being an old-fashioned, shouting Methodist, raised the shout and her oldest daughter in the meantime got saved, and there was so much shouting that even the horses got excited. For the lack of a better name for that, we might call it a revival on wheels.

"When Mt. Carmel School started in September I was able to go back to school. The fall revival began in October. The first night of meeting I was the first seeker at the altar. It took me about a week to get to the point where I met every condition. When I did, God filled my soul with 'joy unspeakable.' I did not feel like the same person. Even my work was different, in that it was a delight to me. With such an experience as this, some folk would think that one would not feel the need of anything else, but in less than two days God revealed to me the need of being sanctified wholly as a second definite work of grace. My heart was open for all the Lord had for me and I sought Him for the experience. Just as definitely as He saved me, He cleansed my heart from carnality and the Holy Spirit came in His sanctifying power. More than a year after that He definitely, beyond any doubt, called me to preach His Word. Instead of it's being something undesirable, now it was a great blessing to me.

"The second time I went home for a short visit, after having been saved, one of my brothers who is older than I, was converted and has been a monument of grace set up before the people ever since. That has been nine years ago now, but we are thankful for the keeping power of the Lord which has kept us both from ever backsliding. Soon after my brother was saved, my mother and other members of the family were seeking the Lord. From time to time as the way has been opened some of my sisters have enrolled in the Mt. Carmel High School. I am convinced that if the Lord lays it on one's heart to go to school and get prepared for His service, and if he will obey, whether he has a dollar in the world to start on or not, God will provide a way somehow. Halleluiah! My soul is blessed afresh as I write about these things. We say with the Psalmist, 'The Lord hath done great things for us: whereof we are glad.'

"After finishing my high school work at Mt. Carmel and taking two years of Bible training at the Kentucky Mountain Bible Institute, I graduated in the spring of 1934. Soon after that I went out to a preaching point. Part of the time I had a young man to work with me, and some of the time I was alone. After a short time at that, I began to help in the carpenter work for our Kentucky Mountain Holiness Association. This consists of building churches, parsonages, dormitories, etc. In the meantime I have held revivals and have done numerous other things that enter into the life of a missionary. The power of God is being mightily manifested and souls are coming to Him for regeneration and sanctification. I do not ask for anything better than that the Lord will let me burn out for Him in winning lost souls in my own native hills."

ANOTHER WRITES:

"In the fall of nineteen hundred twenty-five, when I was not quite fourteen years old, the Lord sent conviction to my heart and I was a miserable little girl. None of my family could understand what was wrong with me because I was acting so differently.

"One Sunday morning my mother and step-father went to visit a sick man, leaving me in charge of my younger brothers and sisters. I, being the oldest of nine children, was taught early in my life to carry responsibilities. Before they went, Mama asked me if I was sick and I said 'No.' That day some of our cousins had come over to play with us, but they played without me.

"My brother took the group of children into the old smokehouse to play 'meetin',' as we called it. I had put a fire in the stove and was going to the smokehouse to sift cormeal. The children had finished their song service and were ready for prayer. My brother was taking charge of the service and, of course, when I entered 'the meeting' he said, 'We'll call on Sister Eunice to lead us in prayer.'

"The Lord struck those words to my heart and I said, 'I believe I can pray!' I fell down by an old broken chair and began pouring out my heart to God in prayer. The children thought that I should have been to the end of my prayer long before I was. Not understanding, my brother went to our neighbors to get them to come and see what was the matter with me. They were gone. God had it all fixed so that there was no one to bother or to hinder me. After about two hours of sincere prayer, God came into my heart and the old world looked different. I found myself out in the yard shouting God's praises.

"Within my own heart I had battles that caused me much unhappiness. The only way I ever kept saved was to pray for forgiveness. When I had done things which were wrong, I would ask the person's forgiveness. Everybody was saying that holiness was a new doctrine and that those who preached it were false prophets.

"The day came when I was to go to Mt. Carmel High School. When I got there, a revival was in progress. The minister was preaching holiness as a second definite work of grace. I did not know very much about the experience except what had been said in opposition to it. The next morning in chapel my heart was so hungry to be sanctified that I was standing with a grip on the seat before me and I was saying over and over, 'Lord, if you ever make me feel this way again I'll go to the altar if it kills me.'

"Realizing that my people did not believe in holiness (some of them believe in it now), it was hard to go to the altar. Miss McConnell and one of the girls came and spoke to me. Finally, I moved my feet around and the next thing I knew I was at the altar praying for the Lord to take carnality out of my heart. He did, and I am praising God from the depths of my soul, as I write this, because He ever put conviction on my heart and then that He led me into this good way of holiness.

"The testings came on every hand from friends and from the church which I had joined. The church people told me I had deviated from the doctrine and asked me to make a statement to clear myself. The deep peace of the indwelling Holy Spirit helped me more than I can ever tell, and I determined by God's grace never to go back on anything that He had done for me. I told them that holiness was as old as the Bible, and I would never deny it. I also told them they could put me out of the church if they wanted to do so. After a few years one of these men turned around and encouraged me to preach it and live it.

"A number of months after the Lord sanctified me I was kneeling in prayer for another person, when the Lord definitely spoke to my heart and called me to be a missionary in my own native hills. The Lord answered prayer and took me through high school. Then He took me through the Bible School at Vancleve. No one was back of me in finances, but through prayer and faith in God, He supplied my every need and saw me through.

"For the past five years I have been out in station work answering the call that God gave me, telling others about this great salvation. In these stations, we live by faith, and our hearts are blessed as God answers prayer for food, clothing, and other things, as He sees we have need.

"As I look back over my life, 'I am persuaded that neither death, nor life, nor angels, nor principalities, nor powers, nor things present, nor things to come, nor height, nor depth, nor any other creature, shall be able to separate us from the love of God, which is in Christ Jesus our Lord.' (Romans 8:38, 39). And my testimony is like that of the Psalmist when he says, 'The lines are fallen unto me in pleasant places; yea, I have a goodly heritage."

ANOTHER TESTIMONY AS FOLLOWS

"To get to my home from Mt. Carmel you go through War Creek, Bloody Creek, then to Devil's Creek; beyond that is Hell Creek and still farther on is Hell-Fer-Sartin Creek, but it was on Devil's Creek where Jesus found me. From my bedroom window I could hear the gray foxes bark from cliff to cliff and could hear the moonshiners chop their wood at night. Some of the cliffs were smoked black underneath where they had put off 'runs.'

"When I was sixteen years of age I had been to 'meetin' seven times. My heart became desperate under conviction and I knew not the trouble. For months I would hurry to bed at night, pull the covers over my head, and pray for mercy as best I knew how.

I suffered and struggled, in ignorance of God's good salvation. One night as I was doing the chores, the Holy Ghost whispered to me that I could get that awful burden off my heart if I would go to my room, get down on my knees beside the bed and pray long enough. I hurried to my room, started praying about dark and prayed until almost midnight. I promised the Lord all I knew to promise; I prayed with my face buried in the sheets; I raised my face toward heaven and prayed; I walked the floor with my hands raised to heaven and begged for salvation; then again I would kneel, burying my face in the sheet. Finally, Jesus began speaking to me. He asked me if I knew how starved I was for salvation. I answered a big YES. He said the folks in the hills were not Christians. He said that some of them were just as hungry for the blessing as I was. Then He asked me if He would save me, would I tell them how they could get saved? My spirit shrank. Mother said if a woman wanted to pray she should get into her closet, shut the door behind her and pray. Father said it was a disgrace for a woman to speak in public. The agony was still on my soul. I decided that if I promised God the hardest, worst thing I could think up, He would save me. I took my face out of the sheet, raised it toward heaven, and said, 'Lord, I'd be low down enough—I'd even disgrace myself enough—to be an old woman preacher if you'd save my soul!' Something happened! I thought the place was filled with angels but didn't see any. Afterwards I read in the Scripture that 'The angels in heaven rejoice over one sinner that repenteth,' and that 'The angel of the Lord encampeth round about them that fear him.' So the room was full of angels! Next morning I went downstairs and looked in the mirror to see if I looked different.

"Shortly after my conversion, missionaries from Mt. Carmel came to Devil's Creek. Among the many who were saved in the revival was my mother, who shouted and spoke in public.

"They told my two sisters and me of Mt. Carmel High School. We prayed for God to get us there, and in the fall of 1931 He opened the way. We felt like David—we could have run through a troop and leaped over a wall. After being at Mt. Carmel for awhile I saw there was no remedy for carnality but to get rid of it. I went to the altar and prayed hard, and God met my need. The Lord sanctified my soul and made it clean there at the altar.

"One day I heard the faculty praying. They asked God to send in to that school from the mountains of Kentucky the boys and girls who were hungry-hearted and wanted to mind God. The Holy Spirit whispered to my heart that these were the folk who had prayed for me, and that was how I found Him and was led to a good Christian school.

"During my second year God again made it plain that I was to be a missionary in the Kentucky mountains. After I had finished four good years in Mt. Carmel High School and three summers at an outpost station, God saw fit to let me have the training in our Kentucky Mountain Bible Institute. I still did missionary work during the summer and went back to school

in the fall. While at Bible School I met Glen Des-
Jardins from Crosswell, Michigan, whom God had also
called to the Kentucky hills. He graduated one year before I did and was sent out in station work. During
these years of friendship we had at one of our Conferences at Mt. Carmel a speaker who preached on leadings. He said that if it were of God we would have a
good 'inward persuasion' and a good 'outward providence;' that often the seasoned saints of God were our
'outward' providence. After two years of deepening
friendship, when both of us had finished high school
and Bible School, Mr. DesJardins and I felt we could
be better missionaries if we worked together—that
was our 'inward persuasion.' The high school and
Bible School faculties felt the same, and that was a
good part of our 'outward providence.' So a lovely
wedding was planned for us at Mt. Carmel High School.
Other 'outward providences' came as God supplied our
need for the wedding and touched hearts in several
states to send gifts to furnish our little parsonage back
in the hills.

"Now we are in the full swing of missionary work.
We have two preaching points a few miles apart, eight
services each week; preaching services, Sunday
schools, missionary meetings, Wednesday evening
prayer meeting, and children's meetings. The children
gather to sing motion songs, learn Bible stories, mem-
orize Scripture, march and play in the rhythm band,
paint, sew and paste. On the other hand, grownups
gather to sing, pray, study the Word, weep for joy,
and praise God with a real testimony.

"This is the richest life for which two young people could ask. We are grateful for the privilege of ministering to the spiritual needs of those who are hungry-hearted. Our only desire besides keeping our own souls blameless before God, is to become more effective continually in getting folk established in holiness."

ANOTHER TESTIMONY

"My dad is just a poor, hard working farmer in the hills of Kentucky. In his early life he had been a moonshiner.

"Mother was saved during a revival meeting held by some of Miss McConnell's workers in our community. From that time on our home was different. She wanted me to go to Mt. Carmel to high scnool, but Dad opposed my going. When school started, I went anyhow. None at home could help me. Miss McConnell wrote and told me to come on. I took what clothes I had and went.

"From the time I arrived on the grounds at Mt. Carmel High School the Holy Ghost began to convict me of my sins. I began to remember all the mean things I had done. During the revival in October, 1939, God got hold of my heart. My sins weighed down upon me so heavy I could stand it no longer.

"After supper one night, I asked one of the boys to go up in the woods near the campus with me and see if God wouldn't forgive my sins. The load of guilt was too heavy; I couldn't wait for the altar service that night. We went up into the woods and by the side of an old hickory stump, on the night of October 25, God came and pardoned me of all my past sins. The glory filled my soul; God had actually forgiven me. I could hardly believe it; I felt as if I were walking on air; I was so happy just to think I had been saved from all the chains of sin which once had me bound in slavery.

"Soon after I was saved I began to realize that I needed something else. One of the boys had done something I didn't like, and I felt the old spirit of anger boil up within me. I knew a Christian shouldn't be like that. On November 15 of the same year I went to the altar and asked God to sanctify me. My call to preach came before me, but thank God, there was one big 'yes' to God and His will in my heart. I hadn't been at the altar long until the Holy Ghost met my need. He had come in all His fulness and burned out the old 'root of bitterness.' The 'old man' had been killed. I was a new man. God had saved, sanctified and called me to preach. Glory to His matchless name.

"As soon as I was saved I began to pray for God to supply all my needs. He had promised to 'supply all my needs according to His riches in glory.' Once I needed a pair of slippers to wear for Sunday. I told God how I needed them, and just what size it would take. I told Him I was willing to wear the old ones for everyday, if only He would send me what I had asked for. God lived up to His promise. In a few days I received a package with TWO new pair of shoes in it. God had done the 'exceeding abundant above all I had been able to ask or think.'

"Why shouldn't I want to serve a God like this? A God who has been so good to me! I can say from the bottom of my heart, 'My heart is fixed, O, God, my heart is fixed.' I have set myself to do His will; nothing can change my mind and heart. I'll mind God, and preach holiness of heart and life unto God in the Kentucky mountains. Glory to His name."

"I remember. so well one of the first answers to prayer I ever received. I was attending the Mt. Carmel High School in Breathitt County, Ky. Spring had come and in less than two weeks we were to have a special program. The shoes I was wearing were almost worn off my feet, and I had no others for the occasion. Mother sent me a couple of dollars and I sent an order for shoes as quickly as possible. On the day when my shoes should have arrived, I received instead a letter saying it would be at least ten days before they would be shipped. Ten days! It was now less than a week till I would be needing them. This was a good time to prove Matthew 21:22, 'All things whatsoever, ye shall ask in prayer, believing, ye shall receive.' So I went to the Lord about it. Since I was a very young convert and did not understand the Bible very well, I knew nothing else to do but take every word of it literally. So when I read in 1 Samuel, 'He will keep the feet of his saints,' I thought surely that meant He would keep shoes on their feet; I belonged to Him; I needed shoes for my feet; therefore I was trusting Him to supply this need. As a result the Lord very graciously answered prayer in plenty of time for me to have my shoes for the program. I do not know just what happened at the other end of the line, but I do know that He verified His promise in my behalf.

"In my purse I had one dime which some little boys had given me for pressing their suits. I felt somewhat like the woman in the Old Testament who had only a small amount of meal with which to make a cake for herself and her son: when she had eaten that they were expecting to die. Yes, I would spend my last dime and then—what. I went down the stairs one day with my treasure clasped tightly in my hand. Something caught my eye. It was a sign on the bulletin board which read like this: '$2.10 still due on our missionary project.' Two dollars and ten cents, and my dime would reduce it to $2.00 even. Finding the prayer band sponsor, I presented my meager offering. I then made my way over to my room and wept most bitterly. Did the heavenly Father hear those groans? Yes, thank God! He heard and answered. Within a few hours I received the answer—not just one dress, but three, along with some other things I needed. Again God did the 'exceeding, abundantly, above' all I asked of Him. Praise His name! The Lord always works things out well when we pray.

"It was because the faithful Christians at Mt. Carmel High School prayed for me that Jesus came in and transformed my life from unhappiness to holy joy, from fear to perfect love, from turmoil to perfect peace, from death to eternal life. I praise Him because He still lives and answers prayer.

"God has very graciously supplied all my needs through Mt. Carmel High School and two years of

Bible training in the Kentucky Mountain Bible Institute. When He first spoke to me through 1 Cor. 9:16,
'Woe is unto me if I preach not the gospel,' I was the
happiest girl in the world to think He would call ME
to be a holiness preacher. But I find that it is not an
easy thing for a Kentucky mountain girl to go out
among her own people and preach, because many of
them believe it is shame for a woman to speak in public. I had my first real struggle along this line a few
weeks after my call was settled. I had gone out to
spend the week-end at one of the out-stations. I had
not expected to be called upon to give a message because I did not know one thing about how to prepare
one; so when one of the workers asked me if I would
preach I refused. I think I would have accepted the
first time if I had known how miserable I would feel
after refusing. As we sat around the fireside that
evening, my heart was heavy. I could understand
something of how Jonah felt when he tried to avoid the
work God had given him to do. The Lord had called
me to preach; He had given me this opportunity; and
I had refused. Finally, I lifted my head and said,
'Well, I will preach tomorrow night.' Immediately I
felt the load lift. I prayed for a text and the words
came to me, 'For the wages of sin is death, but the gift
of God is eternal life through Jesus Christ our Lord,'
but I did not know where they were found. I looked
through the Bible from Genesis to Revelation, but without success. I began to get desperate. I could not
preach from a text which I couldn't find in the Bible.
The people might think I was **giving them** something

which was not Scriptural. I closed my Bible and prayed, 'Lord, if this is the text I am to use, please show me where it is found.' Again I reached for my Bible and opened it at Romans 6:23. I knew then that it was the Scripture He wanted me to use. He gave me a message (I never could have fixed one up by myself) and before I went into the service there was wafted to my heart the comforting promise, 'It is not ye but the Holy Ghost.' That verse has been mine ever since, and the desire of my heart is that I shall always keep in the place where the Holy Spirit can speak through me and use my life to the glory of God.''

I have seen two churches in America that cost one million dollars each. This much money would build exactly 590 churches and 590 parsonages in the long-neglected parts of the Kentucky mountains. And this would just about reach one-sixth of the creeks and branches in the Kentucky mountains alone, not to say anything about the other parts of the Appalachian Highlands. There are six million highlanders in the Eastern part of the United States. Only two million of them have church advantages. These live on the edge of the mountains and in the cities and in the county seat towns. The other four million constitute a great home mission field. Our church buildings are very nice. We are building more of these churches each year. They seat around two hundred. The people are reaching out for the gospel. There are no modernists in the mountains. They love the Bible. If anyone came into this country preaching that there is no heaven or no hell, they would be driven out at the point of a gun, and I would say Amen to it. We pray constantly that no one will ever come back into these hills and mislead the people.

Just as it takes the power of the Gospel in saving and in sanctifying grace in any part of the world to transform lives so that they will stop all sin and live acceptably in the sight of God and man, just so it works in the mountain regions. I was asked to speak some years ago at the International World Convention for the Promotion of Holiness when it met in Chicago. My topic was: "Does Holiness work in the Mountains?" I was able to give a positive answer because the Lord had given us a host of samples in our work who were living a powerful, victorious life right in their community and home.

We have wept and prayed much over such announcements as this in our local paper: "The July term of the Breathitt Circuit Court will convene Monday, July 11, with approximately 450 cases on the docket."

One of our fine men said to me, "Miss McConnell, if you or someone else had come to our creek years ago preaching holiness, I know that most of my children would now be living for the Lord. We got there just in time to reach him and his wife and one of the younger children.

The Circuit Judge said to me one time, "Your work has been able to do more for our country than the law has been able to do in two hundred years." I said, "Judge, to God be all the glory."

CHAPTER V

Up Against The Inevitable

"Ye shall receive power, after that the Holy Ghost is come upon you," Jesus said to His disciples just before His ascension. The Holy Ghost is here officially to serve. He is here to do the work of God, but He works through human agency. He executes God's word through us.

There came a very urgent S.O.S. call across the country from one of our out-station pastors. One of the ladies had an acute attack of appendicitis. Three of us walked four miles. There we got an old Model T. Mr. Myers was the chauffer. After getting some ice in a county seat town, we hastened on through the creeks and the mud. Finally, we came to a very steep hill. We worked hard. After the sixth attempt two of us got out and walked up to the top of the hill where we perfectly agreed in prayer claiming the promise, "Where two of you shall agree on earth as touching anything that they shall ask, it shall be done for them of my Father which is in Heaven." Brother Myers tried it the seventh time and up the hill she came. We thanked God and went on. I know that God put His great hand back of that old car and pushed it up the hill. We were just four hours traveling twenty miles. The Lord had worked at the other end of the line also. We found our patient much improved. The neighborhood folk had applied home remedies and the Lord had used these to give much relief. The mountain people are very versatile in so many ways. Necessity has been the mother of invention. When we left Mt. Carmel we fully expected that we would have to hasten with the patient to Winchester, Ky., to a hospital, which was seventy miles away.

The last of May, 1928, a number of the teachers and myself were attending the commencement at Asbury College. It had rained very hard for nearly three days up at the head of the river. The folk in charge at Mt. Carmel wrote us about the steady rise of the river. We had then our first large swinging bridge across the river. It had cost much. We began at once to pray for the Lord to spare it. A number of summer workers came back with us from Wilmore. When we reached Jackson we were horrified at the fearful destruction that the high waters had made; houses washed away and many people were homeless and sick. At Jackson the little branch railroad called the O. & K. connected with the L. & N. Railroad—for miles it was entirely washed out. What were we to do? We had many suitcases and were twelve miles across country from Mt. Carmel. We walked a mile along the railroad and there camped and prayed. A log raft came down the river which was yet very high. We hailed the men and they signaled to us to come on. The steep, muddy bank was dangerous, but we made it down to the edge of the water, holding on to the roots of the trees and small brush, with mud nearly up to our knees. The men on the raft had a difficult time getting it stopped and close enough to the bank for us to jump on to it. We started on our journey very happy, singing old hymns, and thanking God for His great love and care. Along we went through the woods and around the winding river for twenty-five miles. We said to the men that we had prayed so much for God to save our swinging bridge. They said, "Of course it's gone. We have come fifty miles today and every swinging bridge is gone. Even the big traffic bridge at Haddox is gone." It was located twelve miles above Jackson.

Just at sunset we rounded the last curve which brought us in full sight of the bridge. There she was majestically swinging across the river—clearly seen against the western sky. We cried and laughed and sang the Doxology. This made a deep impression on the raftsmen. We urged them to stay all night with us. While Professor Lauthan and Professor Baldwin helped them to tie up the raft of logs, the rest of us made our way up the Bluebird Trail to Mt. Carmel. Where the river had receded the mud was a foot deep. Our slippers came off as we swished in and out of the velvety path. We trudged on with our baggage, weary, but exceedingly happy in the service of the Lord. We magnified the name of the Lord that night in our family worship. Just at dawn the next morning our kind raftsmen started on their journey down the river one hundred miles to the sawmill to sell their lumber. They said they had been running the river for many years. "Thou calledst in trouble, and I delivered thee; I answered thee," said the Psalmist.

The river with its deep gorges and narrow val-

leys affords much pleasure, but it also is very dangerous. After every high water, every sag and road is
left with deep silt. After one of these spring floods,
Mrs. Swauger was walking from Mt. Carmel to the
mouth of Frozen Creek, there to take the O. & K. train.
She made the mistake of wearing shoes with wide,
thick soles, thinking perhaps she would sort of skim
along on top of the mud which had begun to dry quite
considerably. Every step she took went deep in the
mud. The hot sun and the fearful exhaustion from
pulling her feet out of the stiff mud while hurrying to
make the train, caused her to fear for her life. She
stood on her umbrella while she pulled her feet out of
the mud step by step. She called on the Lord to see
her through. Many have been the narrow escapes of
our workers throughout the Association in these
eighteen years.

The river was full of cakes of floating ice when
one of the boys was setting me across in a large, almost
unmanageable boat. I tried to help the young man by
using a long pole to push the ice away. My strength
gave out. They helped me to the home of Mrs. Noble
on the other side of the river where, with hot applica-
tions and ginger tea, she restored me to consciousness. I shall never forget this kind act of Mrs. Noble.
A Mt. Carmel professor, Mr. R. L. Swauger, came for
me later in the day and our teachers nursed me back
to strength again.

Miss Archer was appointed the Superintendent of
the South and West districts one summer. She started
to visit all of the stations, walking about fifteen miles

one hot day. She tells how if the Lord had not renewed her, she would certainly have gone home to
heaven on that lonely, long trip, where for miles there
was not a house within calling distance. These light
afflictions all worked out for us a far more exceeding
and eternal weight of glory.

Six of us were coming home from Jackson where
we had been attending a revival service. It was rain-
ing; the road off the main highway was in the process
of making. Suddenly the old Dodge car dropped into
the mud to the axles. Mr. Swauger worked and worked to get it out, using rocks, logs, and branches. After
a long time we said, "Let's pray." All of us stood
there in the mud and rain and lifted our hearts to the
Lord in humble faith. We got seated in the car. Mr.
Swauger started it, knowing that the Lord had truly
heard our prayer. The car heaved and jumped out of
the mud. We reached home at one o'clock with the
sweet assurance of the Lord's tangible help. All of us
seem to have so little sense, don't we? No doubt if
we had called on God at the beginning, He would have
answered then.

In the days before the road came through, often
there was no way for us to get our provisions down to
Mt. Carmel from our little freight house at the mouth
of Frozen Creek. Sometimes we would roll a barrel of
coal oil into the river and let it float on the current while the man in the little rowboat, with the
more perishable things, would drift along side of the
barrel. It was an interesting sight for all of us to
watch the boat land at the foot of the Bluebird Trail.

The entire school would come down to carry the goods up the trail a quarter of a mile to the school.

Every time I would see the county Judge in Jackson I would speak to him about making us a road the three miles in from the highway. He would always promise me that he would do all he could to see it through. Sure enough he did. Mr. Swauger and the neighborhood men had made an improvised trail that we could use in the summer time, and so the Judge said any community that was that ambitious should have help. Ours was the first graded road in the county. This time the Lord helped us to work as well as pray. The road was finished in 1933.

Mrs. Elliot heard about our need of a spring wagon at the Hollow Rock camp meeting in 1926. She gave us the money to buy a wagon and a set of harness. The wagon was shipped to Frozen Creek and unloaded in the open. The river was up and there was no way to get the wagon home. We felt the hot sun would soon ruin it. Mrs. Swauger, Miss Archer and I started after it. The men were scarce in those days. They carried the harness across the swinging bridge while Old Beauty and I swam across the river in twenty feet of water. After we crossed Shoal Branch the horse had to climb up a steep, narrow place along the river. The earth gave way and the horse slid down the bank toward the river. Mary and Martha prayed out loud and I held on to the horse's mane and saddle. Beauty struggled up the bank and we went on thanking the Lord for another deliverance. We reached Frozen Station, assembled the wagon, greasing the wheels, etc.

We were all brought up on the farm and knew about such things. It had never occurred to us that Beauty had never been in shafts before and knew nothing about pulling a wagon like that. We finally got her started after much coaxing. We had piled some baggage out of the freight house in the wagon which made the load not too heavy, even with the three of us in the seat. About every ten yards she stopped and would not go. Mary and Martha jumped out and I stood up in the seat trying to make her go by whipping her with the end of the lines. The poor thing was so frightened. She finally reared right straight up in the air until 1 thought she would fall back on the seat with me. After a few of these spells, we decided to let her outdo us and that we could not break her in at this stage of her life. After we tied all of the baggage on her back and got started it was pitch dark, and the rain had swollen all the creeks so that we waded water almost waist deep across White Oak. We left our poor old tired horse on the other side of the river at Mr. Nobles and gave her a good feed, telling her that she need not worry, that we would never try to make her pull a wagon again, but that she would still be our faithful saddle horse.

Many time two of us rode on her back. One time we put a steamer trunk, a tub, a baby organ, and other smaller things on her, but she never balked a bit. One time I tried to lead her across the swinging bridge, but she would not go. Someone said to me, "God takes care of babies and fools." We often take the cows across this bridge which is fifty feet above the water and three hundred and fifty feet long. It is carried by four three-quarter inch cables which are stretched over high pillars on either side of the river. The cables are anchored to dead men, big logs buried twenty feet under the ground at each end of the bridge. The bridge has a floor four feet wide which is laid on two by fours, laid lengthwise of the bridge and fastened to the steel cables by number nine wire. There is a six foot, strong, wire fence strung on each side to keep you from falling off. The bridge is very strong.

On February 5, 1939, the big snow followed by heavy rains caused the river to rise so that the backwater in Frozen Creek made the water to come into our Bible School two miles up the creek. We moved everything to the third story in the main building. The boys' dormitory was almost all under water. These inevitable floods are constantly to be found in the mountains where the tiny, narrow, deep valleys can't take care of the water. Providentially, our darling baby, Lela Grace Myers, was born two weeks before this. Mr. and Mrs. H. P. Myers lived in an apartment in the boys' dormitory at the Kentucky Mountain Bible Institute. We were used to these river floods. At this time our swinging bridge at Mt. Carmel was much in danger. At eleven o'clock some of the students went down to the river. They reported that it was still rising and that the water was within three feet of the floor of the bridge. We committed everything to the Lord and retired for the night. At 2 A. M., I heard a fearful crash from my bedroom window in the girls' dormitory. It was moonlight. I ran down to see, and sure enough the bridge was gone. As I walked up the trail alone, the Lord comforted my heart and assured me He would take care of it all. Every swinging bridge for sixty miles up the river was washed away. The W. P. A. sent word to everyone that they would rebuild every bridge; that money was appropriated for that purpose. The neighborhood rallied to our help so beautifully and our teachers and boys helped. The First National Bank of Jackson gave us the trees for the large pillars which washed away. The "dead men" and the cables were not damaged. In six weeks our bridge was all replaced and better and stronger than ever. All the other bridges were not put up for nearly two years by the W. P. A.

Our day students were crossing the river in a little leaky boat one morning when the boat sank near the bank. All were rescued, but we were in constant fear lest it might capsize in the middle of the river sometime. The boat was used for pleasure on a small lake in a neighboring county and was given to us right after our bridge washed away. It was almost beyond repair then. However, we were so grateful for it because it was in constant use until the bridge was rebuilt.

It is said that an eagle always goes right into the teeth of the storm. If it goes with the storm, the wind will get under its feathers and it will lose control and be dashed to pieces. God has enabled us to face the storm. We are not here for money or ease or worldly fame or comforts, but for souls. While the enemy would try to defeat us, we know that the Lord is stronger than the devil and with the Lord fully on our side we go forward.

"Be ye strong in the Lord and the power of His might,
    Firmly standing for the truth of His Word.
He shall lead you safely through the thickest of the
        fight,
    You shall conquer in the name of the Lord."

The old hymns are sung often in all of our services. "The Son of God Goes Forth to War" is one of the favorites.

"They climbed the steep ascent of heaven
    Through peril, toil and pain:
Oh God, to us may grace be given
    To follow in their train."

We were called to visit one of the out-stations. Miss Genelle Day and I borrowed two horses and started early, knowing it would take us all day. The creek bed was the road most of the way. While we were in the mission cottage, a quick thunderstorm came up. It rained very hard for about twenty minutes. It was time to start back. The creek was like a river. We met some men on the way. They called and said we were brave women and that the road was dangerous. We felt we must go on, sometimes having to let the horses swim through the deepest places. All of a sudden my horse got caught in a deep mirey place. Miss Day screamed out, "Oh, God, take care of Miss McConnell's horse." The horse leaped out on the bank with all fours. We had traveled seventeen miles and reached our destination back at the parsonage. We were very weary.

We were opening up a work in Magoffin County. They arranged for me to speak in the Courthouse in Salyersville on Saturday afternoon. The O. & K. Railroad always furnished me with a pass, so I took the train as far as I could. At a point called Caney, I got a horse and rode fifteen miles farther on. I spoke to a fine, interested crowd Saturday afternoon; then preached at night and had three seekers. Sunday morning I preached again at Burning Fork. I stayed with my dear friends, Alma and Fanny Praeter, for that night and for Sunday dinner. I started back over the hot dusty trail. They had begun to make a new road through that part of the mountains and the dust was very thick. Rarely did I travel alone, but this time it was unavoidable. The enemy came to torment my tired body and mind. I cried and prayed. The fat, lazy horse tried me much. I could not make him go. The devil said, "Nobody cares, and you have no money. If you would die, you would not have even enough to bury you." I prayed and struggled for some time. Finally, I called out, "Mr. Devil, I belong to Jesus and He will see me through." Instantly the promise in Isa. 41:10, "Fear thou not; for I am with thee; be not dismayed; for I am thy God; I will strengthen thee; yea I will help thee; yea, I will uphold thee with the right hand of my righteousness," came to me. My tears were dried. I rode the rest of the journey with the comfort of the Holy Ghost filling my soul. I came into Caney and thanked the man for his horse; ran down the railroad through the dark and stayed in the hotel at Cannel City all night. I took the train early the next morning, got off at Frozen Creek, and walked down the river two miles to Mt. Carmel. Many of our teachers and pastors could relate almost similar stories. Their courage and faith have never failed through dangers seen and unseen.

I am reminded of the day when Miss Archer and I walked twenty-two miles visiting some of the stations. We crossed the hill at Hampton and followed down Nigger Branch until we came to Taulbee Creek. We prayed and testified with the three missionaries and heard their joys and sorrows. Two of these girls were from the city and the other one lived on a farm. One was from Massachusetts, one from Rhode Island, and the other one from Cleveland, Ohio. They were happy in the work even though it was all so new. They had papered the little two-room house with building paper and it looked very lovely and clean. The roof leaked, but they didn't complain. One night a big black snake that was after the mice, dropped from the ceiling into one of their cots. They screamed and it ran out of the house. They had a prayer meeting and God actually delivered them from the fear of it all. They all soon fell asleep and did not awaken until morning. During the summer, five snakes came into their house. Miss Archer and I knew that the Lord had truly undertaken for them.

We proceeded down the creek, jumping across it many times or stepping on the rocks to keep from falling into the water. Our next station was Morgue Creek, where three Quaker girls from Indiana were located. We found them rejoicing in the good victories of their services and their pastoral work in the homes. Here again we had a praise and prayer service. We rested here. We had made the mistake of wearing missionary barrel shoes that were too large. Going up the steep hills we blistered our heels, and going down we wore the skin off our toes. Those pioneer days, filled with rich memories of the Lord's blessings upon the preaching of full salvation, were crowned with many souls.

Dr. G. W. Ridout came to visit us from Wilmore. He was then teaching in Asbury College. The cold March winds had brought a good rain in the night, and unfortunately I had left my horse on the opposite side of the river from Mt. Carmel. In the morning when we were to start on a thirty-eight mile circuit preaching at three points, the river was away past fording. I felt we must go because the people were expecting us. I prayed as I went after "Beauty." This was my first experience of this kind. Some of the folk on the bank said, "Not all horses can swim and the river is dangerous because it is so swift this morning." I felt confident that it was all right and that the Lord's seal was upon it. Mr. Noble got the little boat ready and put the saddle in it. I led Beauty down the slick river bank and got in the boat, all the time coaxing the horse to make the plunge into the muddy waters. All went well and we got over safely and made our appointments on time. Between each meeting Dr. Ridout got his feet and legs perfectly soaked splashing through the creek and roads on our way to War Creek, Oakdale and Chenewee and Elkatawa. His horse was smaller than mine. What a good day the Lord did give us.

These gracious times, when it seemed as if we were up against the inevitable and then to see the mighty hand of God upon us and seeing us through so well, could be multiplied. However, I will relate only two more before I close this chapter.

Luther's Battle Hymn, "A Mighty Fortress is our God" has been our encouragement often. "We will not fear; for God hath willed—His truth to triumph through us."

It was during the second winter of the school that the worst problem came up that we had encountered so far. The young men had come time after time to our meeting from far and near with liquor on their breath so that the atmosphere was filled with it. They would run in and out of the service and drink. One boy even dared to take a drink in the back seat of the church. Things were getting pretty bad. We could not understand it. We prayed, fasted, and pled with the Lord to help us. The shooting of pistols on the outside and the drinking on the campus, troubled our hearts more and more. God was putting it upon us to do something about it. We said, "O Lord, the devil is not going to use his fearful plans to disturb Thy work any longer." The time was ripe and ready for the Lord to use someone to speak with authority. After a hard service one night and the crowd was dismissed, I felt led to step outside where the shooting and drinking young men were. I stood on the front steps and the power of God came upon me, and enabled me to speak with the authority of God's word and the Holy

Ghost. I talked to them about the situation, and said that the devil's power must be broken, and that the Lord was going to control our service more than ever from this time forth, and that the drinking and shooting must stop. One of the dear ladies who lived in the community stepped outside the door and tried to pull me inside saying, "You don't know our boys; they will shoot you." I had no fear; God was upon me. I went on exhorting them. One man nearest to me said, "I have a gun, do you want to see it?" I said, "No, not necessarily." That was the only remark made by the entire group. God used the message for He had given it to me. From that time on things were different, and these young people began to respect the place.

The power of the old-time religion in hearts through prayer is the only remedy for these dear young men. I said to a full house on Sunday night, "Boys, not one of your guns can pick Miss McConnell off. She is immortal until God sees fit to take her home." I pled with them from the platform many times to give their hearts to God and let the Lord clean them up outside and inside. We assured them that we were their true friends and had come to help them if they would only let us. A boy very drunk was disturbing on the outside one night after this. Two other boys were trying to quiet him. I stepped outside and said to the sober boys, "Let us take him off the campus." All of us walked along with him talking kindly to him until we got through the gate. Mrs. Swauger stood watching and praying until I returned in safety. God's power alone sustained us and we were able to put

Him to the test again and again.

In those early days, they went so far as to set off dynamite on the campus. A great host of boys filed into the service very quietly while the preacher was preaching one night. They were very orderly and it occurred to me that something was wrong. All of a sudden a tremendous blast was heard; the building shook. We were all so used to the noise of guns, but this was different. No one stirred, not even the young men who had come in about three minutes before. I soon registered their names in my mind and felt the time had come for us to take some legal methods. The service was dismissed at the regular time and the crowd soon left the campus. We investigated. No damage was done. About twenty feet away from the west side of the main building we saw where the earth had been torn up, caused by the explosion. The neighbors came and said, "You must go to law about this or we won't stand by you any longer because this is dangerous." We did and God used this method to subdue the entire crowd. They spent some time in Frankfort, the capital of Kentucky, where the prison is located. Later they came back, but were friendly and good. One of the smaller boys whom we did not indict because he was so young, wrote to me just last summer and confessed that he too was in the dynamite case, and that now he was seeking God and asked us to forgive him. God has given us a host of them throughout our stations and schools. A young man came to the service one night partly drunk. Later he entered Mt. Carmel High School where the Lord saved him and sanctified him. He is now one of our fine soul winners and has been with us eleven years. He holds three of our diplomas: Eighth Grade, High School, and Kentucky Mountain Bible Institute.

We pressed on claiming the God-given promise, "The mountain shall be thine; for thou shalt drive out the Canaanites, though they have iron chariots, and though they be strong." We can truly say through these many years, having given ourselves to prayer and the ministry of the Word, that the Word of God increased, and the number of the disciples multiplied in the mountains greatly, and a great company of the people were obedient to the faith.

CHAPTER VI

The Pauline Ministry

"As they ministered to the Lord and fasted, the Holy Ghost said, Separate me Barnabas and Saul for the work whereunto I have called them. So they being sent forth by the Holy Ghost departed into Selucia; and from thence they sailed to Cyprus. And when they were at Salamis they preached the word of God." Acts 13, 2, 4 and 5.

The enemy would surely rout us if we tried to work out the Pauline ministry without the sanctifying power that Paul had.

The history of every station is rich in adventure, faith and victory, patient toil, brave endurance, sore trials and seeming defeat sometimes, and yet of victory. The entire major ministry of each station is the salvation of souls and the sanctification of believers, sowing amidst tears and reaping amidst joy.

The out-stations are determined by a number of people in that community writing into headquarters at Mt. Carmel High School asking for a work to be established there. We received one petition with ninety-seven names on it begging us to come and establish a work among them.

Our pastors in these places are two women or a man and his wife who trust God implicitly to supply all their needs. They are like the early Circuit Riders of Methodism. The Association builds the churches and parsonages and furnishes them and takes care of the upkeep, but the workers themselves are living entirely by faith. Hundreds of men and women and young people have been saved and sanctified through their ministry. These outpost stations are a mighty factor toward the evangelization of this long-neglected mountain country of Eastern Kentucky. Many of the young people come to the high school from these stations. Here they become established in two works of grace, and if God lays a call upon their hearts we send them on to the Kentucky Mountain Bible Institute after they graduate from the high school. We have many of these mountain young people, to whom we have given seven years of training, as pastors and evangelists in our Kentucky Mountain Holiness Association. Many pastors in the stations come to us from outside the mountains because they feel led definitely to take up this work in the Home Field among these pure American people. They are attracted by the results they hear and the freedom they are given to work for God in winning souls. This mighty host of well-trained and well established pastors are a sacrificial group whom God is honoring in every way. They carry on these churches with all the dignity and blessing of any city church in America. They take care of the funerals, the weddings, the visitations, revivals, and all regular midweek and Sunday services. These stations are spread over seven different counties and reach tens of thousands of people with the full gospel message. All of the regular pastors are either College trained or Bible School trained, and many of them have both diplomas.

In 1930-'31, the burden for the need of a Bible Training School had become so intense that the Lord in answer to prayer, established our Kentucky Mountain Bible Institute. The property, located at Vancleve in Breathitt County and donated through the kindness of Mr. and Mrs. W. H. Pelfrey had once been an old commissary used by a coal mining company. It was large and well built out of oak lumber. We spent $1250 remodeling it for school purposes, providing for a fine dormitory, class rooms, a large chapel, dining room, kitchen, and pantry. Dr. H. C. Morrison and Rev. Warner P. Davis came and dedicated the building. In 1937 a new dormitory for men was built.

The young people with the call of God upon them felt the need of further training beyond the high school work in order to fit them better for missionary work in their own native hills and this was the solution. Truly the Lord's blessing was mightily upon it. Miss Martha Archer, the principal, and two students opened the Bible School in October, 1931. From then on a steady increase of faculty members and students have come from year to year.

The training is a full Bible course of three years with kindred subjects as Theology, Psychology, Ethics, Church History, English and Speech, Greek, Homiletics, and Music, vocal and instrumental. The entire object of the school is to give young men and women called of God a training that will make them efficient in any line of service. The Bible school is not limited to mountain young people alone. High school graduates from other states find here excellent environment and preparation for whatever God has called them to do.

The teachers in our three schools volunteer their services. They come to us with no salary offered whatsoever. All of them have finished their college work and some of them have their M. A. degree in Theology. They are well qualified, experienced teachers. Most of them have a life call; consequently they are with us year after year. However, new ones are added constantly as the burdens, duties, and enrollment increases. These workers represent twenty-two states and twenty denominations.

This faithful, competent group of sanctified men and women have made the K. M. H. A. what it is. Their Pauline ministry is rich, permanent, and far-reaching. I feel many times that I am the least of them. They do the work, and I just follow along after them and do a little guiding now and then when some hard problem is to be settled. Their vision and burden for souls grows from year to year. The accumulation of visits, services, revivals, Sunday schools, and prayers is telling with a greater harvest of souls each year. Their faithful ministries to the sick and dying and those in sorrow have lifted many heavy hearts. The life of the missionary is very precious because all is done for the glory of God and the salvation of souls.

Like the Apostle Paul, the commission of our missionaries to the mountains is "to open their eyes and to turn them from darkness to light, and from the power of Satan unto God, that they may receive forgiveness of sins, and an inheritance among them which are sanctified by faith that is in me."

In fulfilling this ministry we can in a measure like Paul also say, "Once was I stoned, in journeyings often, in perils of water, in perils of robbers, in perils in the wilderness, in perils among false brethren, in weariness and painfulness, in watchings, in hunger, and thirst, in fastings often and in cold. Beside those things that are without, that which cometh upon us daily, the care of all the churches."

Sometimes we have had the high waters to come into the mission houses so that we have had to vacate temporarily. We had lived through seven floods at our K. M. B. I. up to July, 1939. Getting up in the night to move the cars and other things to higher ground was becoming a common thing. While we were used to floods from the back waters up the creeks from the Kentucky River, we had never had a flood come from the other direction.

About four o'clock in the morning of July 5, a cloudburst on Frozen Creek caused a twenty-foot wall of water to come raging down the narrow valley sweeping everything in its path. Forty-four houses, sixty barns, trees, cattle and rocks were picked up and carried away and dashed to pieces. Fifty-two people lost their lives over a period of less than three hours. There was sixteen inches of rainfall. The precious mountain people suffered a great loss.

Both of our Bible School buildings went with the occupants in them, sixteen in all Nine were drowned.. Bro. Horace Paul Myers from Asbury College had been with us ten years and had given such efficient, tender service. He and his three children; Titus, aged six and

a half; Phillip, aged five; and Lela Grace, aged six
months, all went to heaven early that morning. What
a wonderful reunion they must have had. Elsie Booth,
who had been with us four years and called to work in
her own native hills, knew Jesus well. After the
building fell apart, she was seen floating on the water
singing the Doxology. Her precious little body was
found about twenty-five miles away, but it was in such
a condition that no one recognized her. Later, through
the process of elimination when most of the dead had
been found, permission was given to disinter the body.
Her folk truly identified her and took the remains to
their own home cemetery at Happy Top in Lee County.
She was the only daughter. After the Lord had saved
her at Mt. Carmel High School, on her first visit home
she was able to bring the light to her dear mother so
that she found the Lord. Her beautiful life and testimony made an impression wherever she went. Chris-
tine Holman, another student who had come from
Missouri three weeks before to enroll in our Bible
School, and three visitors from Petersburg, Indiana,
who had come to visit the Myers' family over the
Fourth of July, were drowned. Two of these visitors
were Brother Myers' nieces and the other was a boy
who had come to see if he could enroll in our high
school. All of them knew Jesus well and thus had an
abundant entrance. Betty Mae Myers, the only daughter of Mr. and Mrs. Earl Myers, aged fifteen, was the
only body found in time so that they could take her
home to Petersburg, Indiana, for a real funeral. It
was her first visit to her Uncle Horace and Aunt Net-

tie's home, but she has been visiting Jesus and Uncle
Horace and his three precious children ever since.

Seven out of the sixteen in the buildings got out at
various distances along the creek and river. They
were most miraculously delivered from the raging
waters after floating on pieces of boards and whatever
they could get hold of and sometimes being dashed under the waters and bumping against the rocks and
trees in the narrow gorge of Frozen Creek. One teacher was carried down the creek and into the Kentucky
River ten miles. One of the students got out of the
river eight miles down. Another one was able to grab
a willow bush and pull herself to bank at the foot of
Mt. Carmel campus which was four miles from where
the Bible School buildings were. She landed there at
4:40 A. M. and raised the alarm so that the folk at the
Mt Carmel School went to her rescue and were utterly
shocked to see her crouching at the edge of the woods,
and to learn that everything was washed away. Mrs.
Myers was washed down the creek and then up the
river for three miles, where a man heard her cries and
rescued her. She walked to Mt. Carmel expecting to
see Mr. Myers and the three children. She waited
until three in the afternoon; then she gave up all hope.
She was sustained by the mighty grace of God.

There was no expense connected with any of the
funerals because all were buried in home-made caskets.
The land was donated for our first graves. The men
in the community did all the work of digging the
graves. Mrs. Myers was not able to attend any of the
funerals, but the cemetery is in sight of our buildings

and thus she could see all that was going on from her bedroom window. Day after day as the bodies were found we made a new grave. The body of Brother Myers was fonud in the afternoon of July 9th. We buried him Monday morning at 9:30. The Lord did so marvelously bless and comfort and bring light to dear Mrs. Myers. She is still with us teaching in our new Bible School and so well seasoned in the things of God.

The promises of God never were richer. God was preciously near every hour of the day and night. The gracious seasoning of the Holy Ghost power that had been accumulating in the hearts and lives of our workers through the years was well appropriated in these severe tests and sorrows. The dear friends in Jackson, our county seat, were the first to send us an offering of forty dollars. It came the fifth day after the flood. They have stood by us in many hard places through these years. God bless and reward them much for their kindness to us.

Many folk came to comfort and help us from various states. Others wrote letters which meant much to our sorrowing hearts. Mrs. Myers received hundreds of letters and all but a few of them compared her to Job.

We had just finished paying for the new dormitory for boys and the remodeling of the large administration building of the old Bible School, and now we must begin again to prove the depths of God's love and care for us. This rugged way of faith is truly a strengthening and deepening process in the things of God. Our faith kept sure and steadfast. We understood better the suffering beauty of Calvary.

Folks offered us land here and there. We felt led to accept the very kind offer of Mr. and Mrs. Fred Fletcher and their sister, Laura. The three-acre site is beautiful. It is located on a high hill overlooking the river far above the danger of any high waters. It is located on the Mt. Carmel road half way between state highway No. 15 and the headquarters of the Association at the Mt. Carmel School.

God touched hearts over this nation and around the world to send money so that the largest and main building was completed enough for us to begin school October 20th of the same year. Men came from various sections of the mountains and other states and rallied to our need. God enabled us to believe for the money, and with the gracious help of those who volunteered with labor, the work moved on very fast. We were able to use the same gas well by piping the gas two and a half miles.

The second building, which contains a large and beautiful chapel, boys' rooms, and music rooms, is now finished. We all felt led to dedicate the chapel in memory of our dear Brother Myers. The service was one long to be remembered. God had given Mrs. Myers a special lift in her soul the night before, as we prayed with her and comforted her. "Earth has no sorrow that Heaven cannot heal."

The entire cost of rebuilding, counting everything, the volunteer help, the food bills, hauling bills, chapel seats, furnishings, piping gas, etc., was over $32,000. We praise God that in less than three years he has answered prayer and cleared the entire debt. On the door of each room there is a brass plate bearing the names of the kind friends who donated the money for the furnishings.

Dr. and Mrs. H. C. Morrison stood by us so graciously. They gave us all the space we wanted in *The Pentecostal Herald* to let our friends know about our sorrow and the rebuilding. Dr. Morrison sent us a gift and said, "I want to put my old shoulder under your heavy burdens." We thank God for their understanding and vital interest in this holiness work of faith ever since its beginning.

While the Red Cross could not help us to rebuild because we were an institution, yet our hearts rejoiced to know how well they cared for the dear people in Breathitt County who had lost their loved ones, houses, crops, and gardens. We prayed much for the Lord to help and comfort them for we knew so many of the families who were broken up.

A Macedonian call from the people in a needy community in Lee County had been coming to us for three years. We at last could answer it. After much praying and correspondence in order to secure the proper workers, we felt led to take a lady from North Dakota and one from Canada, both well fitted in head and heart for the work. They went the day before in order to help the ladies of the community get the little parsonage ready to move into. We started out early in the morning with the old Dodge and the trailer filled to the limit with furnishings, etc. Mrs. Swauger drove the car. Three high school boys went with us. We got along very nicely the first forty-eight miles; then we came to a very narrow place in the little hillside trail on a steep incline. The rain which had fallen in the last few minutes had made the road very slippery. Nevertheless, we tried the chains and the help of the boys to make it. We soon found that it was impossible. We called to some men near by. They came and helped us to the top of the hill. They told us that it would be impossible for us to go on. The road was too slick and the hills too steep and long. We rested in the nearest home which was Mrs. Angel's. We said to her. "How far is it yet to where the missionaries are going to live?" We were standing on the porch. She put her hands on her hips and looking in that direction said, "Law, honey, it is way the tether side of yander." We found out that it was nearly six miles yet to the little cottage. The Angels said they would find a team and wagon. They secured a mule from one man and a wagon and mule from another. We could just get one-half of the things in the wagon. They started and reached the place at 6:00 P. M. The ladies were there waiting for the stove and the tin to mend the roof. The next day the two Angel boys took the rest of the furniture which we had stored over night in their home. It was a very fine station and many found the Lord.

I asked the missionaries not to give an altar call for the first three months because it was a new station and the people needed to be taught first and indoctrinated. Finally, one Sunday morning they asked if anyone wanted to get saved. Instantly three mothers came to the front seats of the little schoolhouse and prayed for the Lord to forgive them. In a short time two of them came through; the other one did not get saved then, but did later. One of them said she had prayed long before daylight for the Lord not to let it rain that day. She said if it had rained her husband would not have let her come the four miles over the mountain carrying her baby. She was so thankful because the Lord had come into her heart. She said it was the first opportunity in her life that she had to find the Lord.

God's keeping power in times of distress is rich. We have learned that it is possible to take the spoiling of our goods joyfully. Two of our young men were robbed of all their best clothing one summer. At another station the girls were relieved of their fountain pens and other valuables from the cottage, while they were conducting the Sunday morning services up the creek about a half mile from their house. About midnight a man came in through the open window and searched all through the missionaries' things, looking for money. One of the girls was awakened by the noise. She was so frightened she could not call the other lady who was sleeping on the other side of the room. God put the song, "Elijah's God still lives," on her heart in order to help her nerves. She sang it all the way through. God used it to convict the man of his terrible crime. The missionary heard the robber go to the bookcase where they kept the missionary offering. She prayed for God to protect this money because it was all sacrificially given. He left without taking anything or doing any harm.

About 7:30 one night in March, we heard a fearful crash over at the Mt. Carmel garage which is located across the river about one-eighth of a mile from the campus. We had a large six cell flashlight which we flashed over the river from the main building. It lighted up the whole situation. They answered us back with six shots. We heard the bullets whiz through the trees. None of them hit us. The robbers left without anything that night. Later in the year they came back and took all four wheels with the tires of our pick-up Chevy truck. Salvation heals every wound and helps you to love folk and pray for them regardless of the sins they commit against you.

But the word of God grew and multiplied as in Paul's day. Station after station was permanently established. Young people in larger groups were found in these isolated sections who came to Mt. Carmel where they found God's plan for their lives. The far-reachedness of this Pauline ministry cannot be estimated. Aggressive Christianity gets a mighty grip on a country where Holy Ghost filled men and women live before the people, preach a full gospel, and thus defeat the power of darkness and unbelief.

At Lee City, one of our older stations, the people kept asking us to start a grade school which we did. It has been the means of helping a host of children through the grades. The teachers feel fully repaid by the results they see. The pupils are getting a training not only in their books, but in their hearts, which will follow them all through life.

Misses Carter, Humphrey (now Mrs. James Keysor) and Paulo had charge of the church and work at Lee City for many years. Their faith and untiring labors among the people, eternity alone will reveal. To hear the Christians pray and testify is enough to repay us all for the years we have been working in this tiny settlement far back in Wolfe County along the headwaters of the Red River.

They were conducting services at their second charge when a young man came into the schoolhouse smoking. One of the kind gentlemen, who was a deputy sheriff, spoke to the young man about it and asked him to quit smoking inside the building. At once the boy drew his pistol on the man. Miss Carter jumped between them and said, "Don't shoot this man. He is a friend to us and here to protect us. If you must shoot, shoot me. I'm ready to die and the sheriff is not." The boy left the house. They went on with the service. Presently he came in again and walked up to the man and said, "Now I am going to kill you." This time Miss Humphrey and Miss Carter dropped on their knees and asked the Lord to help. Miss Carter cried out, "Oh Lord, take charge of this situation." By this time folk were running out the door and jumping out the windows. God surely did answer their prayers. While five shots were fired, no one was killed and no one hurt except for a slight skin wound on the arm of the boy. That ended the service for the day. The next Sunday the services continued as usual. The sheriff with his family, lived near the church. A little later this deputy, who is past fifty, sought the Lord and found Him precious to his soul. He lives and testifies so good. He tells how the Lord forgave him and how later He took carnality out of his heart and delivered him from the power of sin.

A few years ago while one of our boys was conducting a revival, a man near by was trying to break up the meeting by selling moonshine whiskey to the boys who attended the meeting. Things became very serious. Our mountain boy said he was not afraid. God overruled and ten people sought the Lord. The devil's power was broken. The moonshiner cried out for mercy and asked the evangelist to pray for him.

One of the preachers who lived there was brought under deep conviction through the ministry of this mountain boy. He testified how he had really known the Lord a few years ago but had backslidden and was living in deep sin. He said the Lord had shown him in this revival that folk do backslide and get far from God and finally are lost. He had heard the teaching "once in grace, always in grace." He came to the altar confessing his need and the Lord was faithful to His promise, "Return unto me and I will return unto you saith the Lord." If we haven't sinned away our day of grace the Lord will have mercy on us. "The ministry and apostleship, from which Judas by transgression fell, that he might go to his own place," is the lot of many men and women today.

This place was known for much disorder. One night a year before this another man was holding a meeting in this community and the boys in order to hinder the meeting threw a dead polecat in the window. The evangelist threw it out; the boys kept pitching it in. Finally the preacher threw it in the stove which of course made a bad matter worse.

Brother Howard Paschal and the Old Time Religion Tabernacle had us come to Ft. Wayne and help him broadcast in order to build a church for us on Devil's Creek where we have an out-station. The money came in so well that we were able not only to build our love·ly church called the "Old Time Religion Chapel" on Devil's Creek, but also to build a parsonage at Consolation, another one of our out-stations, and pay $600.00 on our food bills. We praise God for this and for all who contributed.

In this place before the church was built, we were holding a revival. The boys backed a mule up beside the schoolhouse and made it kick. Others were throwing rocks on the roof and at the sides of the building. While this was going on, one of our timid sanctified men got blest and shouted. Others got blest and through it all five people were at the altar praying through. The preacher, who was Mattie White, one of our splendid mountain girls whom God uses mightily to conduct revivals, had to stop preaching, but the Holy Ghost carried on the service. It is rich to see God work. The Lord helps us to hold on and never beat a retreat and leave the field to the mercy of the devil "Through God we shall do valiantly, for he it is that shall tread down our enemies."

"And the word of the Lord was published throughout all the region. And the disciples were filled with joy and with the Holy Ghost."

Invariably we dedicate our churches on a Monday so that the faculty and students who want to go can, since we never have school on that day. From all over the Association and from the surrounding community folk come on horse back, in jolt wagons, or on foot. Recently many come in their cars since there are more roads.

On one of these occasions we had Brother L. O. Florence and Professor Puntney of Wilmore, and Miss Elizabeth O'Conner of the Oakdale Free Methodist Mission, to take part in the service. A truck load of us from Mt. Carmel went fifteen miles to the train. After going twelve miles by train we were met by a truck and taken three miles where we got out and walked about a quarter of a mile to the River. All of us took off our shoes and hose and forded the river on foot. The happy crowd saw the church in the distance only a mile away. Dinner was served in the church-yard around a lovely spring of cool water. The bright October sun added much to the blessings of the day. The pastor and his wife were such good hosts. The messages, testimonies, and special singing caused our hearts to rejoice in the God of our salvation. Much praise was given to the Lord for His goodness in planting one more Lighthouse in Breathitt County.

The people of this community have been hidden away from the outside world until the last six years so that the workers had many things to overcome in laying a foundation for a revival. Soon the children became interested, then some of the grown ups, and then a good revival. Over a period of twelve months the

missionary offering was $10.00 and every cent of it
was given in pennies except what the missionaries
themselves gave. They love to give what they can.

In a community where the teachings of Alexander
Campbell are so prevalent, we dedicated a church.
(You will remember that Campbell founded a church
that denies the third person of the Trinity. Dr. W. B.
Godbey, that great Kentucky commentator and fine
Greek scholar who was so well sanctified by the Holy
Ghost, challenged Campbell on more than one occasion). During the service I read out of the Methodist
discipline, "We dedicate this church in the name of the
Father." I then had all the people repeat it in the audience and the church was crowed. I then read and
had them repeat, "We dedicate this church in the name
of the Son." When they all repeated the last sentence,
"We dedicate this church in the name of the Holy
Ghost," a wave of glory swept over the place through
the rich presence of the Holy Ghost Himself. I shall
never forget it. It did not dawn on me until some
time later why this heavenly breeze at this part of the
service. Then the Lord revealed to me how the dear
people had been deceived and now when they had thus
honord the Holy Ghost He had manifested Himself to
them in this rich and tangible way to cause them to
weep and the saints to shout for joy, for we already
had many converts along that creek.

At the time of the writing of this book we are planning to dedicate our new church at Taliega in Lee
County. Here the people have helped much with labor
and funds. Rev. and Mrs. James Keysor are carrying

on the work here. God has just given them a revival where twelve people were converted and then sanctified.

The best people are always interested in getting a work of God established firmly in their community. Brother H. L. Henry and his wife lived at Index when we opened a mission there in the early days of the work. They gave us an acre of good land in a fine location. They said they wanted to give us the best they had. Today we have one of our finest groups of men and women. Soon after the work started, Brother and Sister Henry sought the Lord. Brother Henry said he had failed God while he was a student at Berea College years before this. God had called him to preach. He said, "I have paid dearly for my failure." He got back to God in good shape and has been a strong preacher of full salvation in heart and life ever since. We elected him president of our board of trustees. He has been stricken with Tuberculosis, but oh, so victorious in his soul.

In order to give the reader a more tangible idea of the kind of work done by our pastors I will let one of our young women tell you.

"I count it a privilege to have spent the past ten years in the Kentucky Mountain Holiness Association. It has been wonderful to see God answer prayer during my training at the Kentucky Mountain Bible Institute in preparation to better answer my call to preach to the people of 'my own native hills,' and during the years since, when I've been out in full time station work.

"God led me to Mt. Carmel High School in 1930 where I took some post-graduate work for one and one-half years. It was three days after going there that God called me to preach. It was also while I was still there that I felt my call was to the Kentucky mountains and that I should spend my life helping in this faith work which Miss McConnell had established. Some of my friends advised me to take up something else in life that would mean a good paying salary, but I found greatest peace when I settled it that I would give my life in His service.

"I had never been used to a lot of luxuries that many enjoy, having been raised on a mountain farm where not many of those things can be afforded, or it might have been harder for me to submit to God's will in the matter of going without a salary.

"I had my first experience of station work in one of our permanent stations as a summer worker. I had the nice sum of $7.00 or $8.00 to live on that summer. That was a lot! The ghost of starvation could make no impression on me that summer with that much money in my pocket book. The biggest battle I had that time was feeling so inferior to the workers I was placed with—I was younger in years and much less experienced than they. After several days of terror along that line, I went to my room and talked to the Lord about it. I told Him I felt inferior and inexperienced but that He had called and I would do just the best I could. The victory was won. The summer was blessed. The first night I preached a young man was gloriously sanctified in spite of my being so inexperienced.

"The following summer I was sent to the same station. I recall no special trials. I had been trusting God for food and clothing, but the third summer the fires of testing came. I went to the station with an empty pocket book. God had not seen fit to send me any money from any source as yet, for the summer provisions. I said nothing to anyone but trusted God. I got a taste of real living by faith that summer. All we had to eat for days was molasses and bread—molasses being a food I never relished so much, especially without having butter. I found grace to help me to relish that diet more than I could have ever dreamed. Of course, I will admit I had some battles in the meantime when meal after meal was the same. The devil whispered over and over, 'If you were in Gods' will you wouldn't have so little to eat.' I almost found my-self taking sides with him occasionally, but I did not allow myself to doubt God, so kept praying and believing Him. Not once did I feel like running away to get a job to make money to buy the necessities. I had such peace in obeying God and staying in His will that I'd rather starve than to have the peace go from me by disobedience. In due season prayer was answered and we had other things added to our food supplies. Miss McConnell always tells us not to go out and starve, if we need anything to write in for it.

"I recall another instance when our flour can was empty and I read of some one who sang the doxology in the empty flour barrel and God sent flour. I thought it might work in my case and it did. The experiences are far too numerous to mention how God has so remarkably answered prayer for food, clothing, and even postage stamps. I was praying for money for a coat one time and a woman told me later she was disturbed at night about sending some money to help me buy one.

"I count it by far the greatest joy to have witnessed answer prayer for the salvation of the souls of our children, young people, and fathers and mothers.

"It has been proved numberless times unmistakably, that God honors a definite holiness ministry. In our revivals where holiness is stressed constantly and strongly, believers get sanctified, sinners fall under conviction and the saints are edified.

"Recently the Lord gave us in one of our children's meetings in our station a real revival. The meeting was being held on a Friday afternoon while school was still going on. The schoolteacher was always appreciative of our work with them and co-operated well. This gave us much more liberty in working with these young lives. It was my time to give the message that particular afternoon. I went with a special burden and prayed for God's blessing on this service. I've always felt a lack of ability to work with children and many times felt I would be justified in shifting the responsibility on someone who was more adapted. God used that message to bring conviction. All during the service I was conscious of the special blessing of the Lord and saw conviction settling down. Not knowing the schoolteacher very well, I hesitated to give an altar call. I asked for hands for prayer and many were raised in response; then I dismissed with a prayer for them. The teacher came to the front in tears and exhorted the children to give their hearts to Jesus until she was overcome by tears. Then I felt the way open for an altar call and all except one girl about sixteen years old responded. Many knelt by their seats, some leaning on their desks. There was weeping all over the house and it wasn't long until they began to get the victory one by one. One little fellow was soon going from one to another as an altar worker telling them what God had done for him and what He would do for them. The blessed part of it is that after several months we still hear of how these children are praying and loving the Lord. Most of them live so far from the schoolhouse where we have our regular services, that they cannot always get there. Our parsonage and land on which to build is located much nearer the community where these children live and that is one reason why we are so zealous to have a church built.

"This station has been open for five or six years. The parsonage has been built for a few years and we feel definitely the Lord wants to give us a church this year. A small start has been made. Some logs and labor have been donated and we believe they are going to give more yet in the way of labor, logs and perhaps money. They are not financially able to give very much. My heart was encouraged a few weeks ago with a definite move in answer to prayer concerning money for the building fund. I became concerned because things were moving so slowly about our building. I felt I should fast and pray one morning which I did. The week passed; no money came. The enemy taunted by saying, 'It doesn't look as if your prayers and fasting amounted to anything.' But praise the Lord, the next week I received notice of $50.00 which had come from some friends in Ohio designated for the Consolation Church. God answers prayer."

In a very short time the prayers of this faithful pastor and others were answered for the Consolation Church. Dear Mrs. Houck, of Ft. Wayne, Ind., sent $700.00 to make it a memorial to her beloved husband. By the time this book is printed the church will be completed. It is built differently than most of our churches. It has folding doors in the back for Sunday school rooms and a small hallway as one enters. It blesses our hearts to go through the mountains and see in the distance a church with a belfry. They are indeed lighthouses where the entire community could find the Lord if they would. Our Sunday schools are a mighty factor for God. This generation of young people in these neighborhoods are getting the Word of God so their outlook on life and standards will be different.

Young people from other states come to us for their Bible School work. During their three years of study and practical work in our stations over the week-end or in the summer time, they see the great need of the country. God has laid His hand on many like this for life service in the Kentucky hills. Another one of our pastors tells of his experiences in this Pauline ministry:

"To be a missionary in the Kentucky mountains one must have a determination to mind God, backed up by the presence of the Holy Ghost. This determination will be severely tested especially in the beginning of one's experience as a missionary.

"In the fall of 1936 I went to Bryant's Creek station for my first time as a permanent pastor. The preceding two years I had assisted in week-end meetings and Sunday schools while in school at the Kentucky Mountain Bible Institute and during the summer. Never in my life had I cooked an entire meal, but I came fortified against that necessity with four recipes; for biscuit, cornbread, gravy, and cocoa. I figured I could survive with that knowledge. The headquarters of the work made it plain that I was to get what I needed at the nearest store and charge it to them. Down in my heart I said this would be a good opportunity for me to test my faith and see if I could live without their support, as the other workers did. So I decided I would keep that burden to myself and trust God to take care of my needs some other way.

"With that in mind I went to the little two-roomed 'parsonage' up on the side of a hill almost out of sight of any neighbor. Six months were spent there. I carried on the regular station work and that experience was invaluable. I was tested and tried along every line; food was scarce, I ran out of coal, was lonely, and it seemed as if the heavens were brass when I prayed. Finally, the last few weeks my own soul was blessed and comforted, even though I saw but little change in the community. About the first of June I left, in somewhat the same manner as did one of the church fathers leave his hermitage, with a cultivated spirit, but injured digestion. One fact was impressed on me—that was the need of living and preaching a heartfelt experience of holiness. The trumpet of my life and preaching must not give forth any uncertain sound. The fall of 1937 another young man and I came back to Bryant's Creek, tore down, and rebuilt the house with an extra room. The house is now on the church site. We prayed much and God graciously undertook and laid it on the hearts of the community to do the hauling free of charge. When the house was in shape, a group came from our Bible School and High School and papered each room.

"November 26, 1937, I was married. It was not so hard to suffer hard things alone, but with a wife, it was a different proposition. However, the Lord never failed us. The food supply was low at times, but our needs were supplied. We never were as low as when I was alone. Even though we had no salary, He supplied our needs from fifty to sixty sources. Some whom we had never seen, would send an offering.

"But we were not in missionary work to make a living. We wanted to help people—help them find God. Regularly we prayed for a gracious revival, and the 'mustard seed' began to grow. When we had been there but a few months, the Lord began to burden our hearts. We prayed and felt around carefully and saw He wanted us to carry on a definite line of Bible study for our personal edification. This marked an epoch in our experience. The prayerful and systematic study of the epistles especially convinced us afresh as to the need of preaching holiness as a second definite work of grace.

"Our prayer still was that God would make us 'increasingly useful.' In January, 1939, there came a Macedonian call from another community, Mill Branch, about four miles distant. We were already carrying on from four to six services weekly, as well as having fencing, painting, building, and gardening to do. But we felt this to be an unusual pull so we began Sunday school there in the afternoon.

"One needed strong faith and legs to make the trip. The path and creek bed were steep and rough, and in winter the creeks were so full it was a serious problem to get there. I learned to jump and scramble and keep my footing like a mountain goat. The creek bed would be full, with steep inclines and cliffs on either side. One had to edge along the stream part of the time, dodge under cliffs and falls, and keep balanced on the inclines by holding on to brush and trees. I went alone. It was too far for my wife. A few times she rode, but it was rather dangerous.

"To this community the gospel was new, and as the Sundays came and went I could see conviction settling down upon hearts. The Lord was using the truth. The time came for a revival, and in spite of warnings that our services would be 'torn up,' we went ahead and had a successful meeting. One young mother had been converted before the meeting, and conviction came mightily upon her husband. Finally, one night after a number were already at the altar, he came fairly running and soon prayed through. He went home, threw away a number of cheap story magazines, and got rid of his pistol. We gave him a Bible as a substitute, and the last time I was there it looked as if it had had plenty of use.

"In about six months we announced another meeting with a young man, a graduate of the Mt. Carmel High School and Kentucky Mountain Bible Institute, as evangelist. Conviction settled in after a few nights, and souls began seeking. One prayed through in her home, and where she had been full of doubts and had questioned the experience of holiness, she now bore fruit in a testimony full of joy and confidence.

"I had been walking home every night after the service. The first two nights a shower of rocks greeted me as I started home. Most of them missed by a pretty good margin, so I did not think anyone would injure me deliberately. As we knew the boys were rather rough, we had said very little about order, knowing that would make matters worse. But the third night as I was finding my way carefully along a narrow path, full of projecting tree roots, I saw that in spite of precaution some one was bent on hitting me, for rocks and stones were coming very close. I did the wisest thing I knew to do, and walked along as if nothing was happening. I had learned by experience never to show any fear. Suddenly a stone caught me just above the ear. Whether I fell down or not, I don't know. I got home all right but failed miserably trying to conceal it from my wife. I was put out of commission as far as the revival was concerned for three nights. The evangelist carried on by himself and had no trouble. There was no trouble after I went back, for a few nights, and then it started again. They did everything they could think of to scare us out, but we held on and the meeting closed with good success. The Lord over-ruled. I began concentrating my prayers on the young man that I was quite sure had hit me, and in about ten months he confessed to me that he was the one who had hit me with a rock and said he was 'awful sorry.'

"For three years we labored at the Bryant's Creek station. The station was built up in interest and attendance, and indifference was being broken down,— but still no souls for Jesus. We prayed much. The third year we laid hold on God afresh and announced the meeting. I felt led to set aside one-half hour every day outside of our regular means of grace to pray for the meeting, about two weeks before it was to begin. From that I got Romans 5:20, 'Where sin abounded, grace did much more abound.' I felt encouraged. The meeting began and went on a few nights, and souls began to seek Jesus. From then on we had an altar service every night except one. At one service ten were seeking for either conversion or sanctification. That was in September, 1940, and when we left there in April to go to another station, the majority were still holding true. Some of them especially showed real transformations of character. How their faces did shine! Surely 'twas heaven below.' The Lord does honor persistence when we are in line with the Spirit.

"The positive, unashamed reverence the mountain people have for the Scriptures is a great help in getting a wedge of truth into their hearts. As soon as we have a group of converts, we organize a course in

Bible study. It feeds their souls, strengthens their faith, and they get the great truths of salvation clear in their minds. That plan was laid on our hearts when we were praying about how we could get the new converts better established in holiness.

"Their testimonies showed plainly how firm a grip the truth of holiness was getting on their hearts. One testified that after she had been saved a short time she felt like she was 'a-smothering' and too, she lacked courage in taking a stand in her home, but after the Holy Spirit came into her heart she had light and liberty, neither was she afraid to kneel before her family beside her bed before she went to sleep. Hardly a one failed to mention the incoming of the Holy Ghost into their hearts—yet *some had never heard it preached before.*

"In that location we had to live by faith in more ways than one. Our usual means of travel was by rail, on foot, and horseback. The railroad station was about three and a half miles away from home with a river between. We crossed the river by boat, so the problem also was, will the boat be on the right side? When the river was low I could wade across and get the boat, or if there was no boat at all, wade and carry my wife. So when the river was up, all we could do was pray that we would find the boat waiting. During the three and a half years we were at Bryant's Creek station, we never missed the train. We did our best, and the Lord helped where we could not do anything. Once my wife, her sister and I were on our way to the station, and when we were yet a good way off we heard the whistle. I began running—with a box in each hand and a suitcase 'harnessed' on my back. The train began to pull out of the station, so I made a short-cut, ran up a bank, pulled through high weeds and briars, and came out on the track just as the locomotive was approaching. I was praying, and so were the folk behind, and the engineer looked out and saw a rain-soaked, box-covered man trying to signal, so he put on the brakes. We climbed aboard, thankful we did not have that long walk back in the rain.

·   "There are so many things that could be told in detail as definite answers to prayer: how God raised up friends, some whom we had hardly seen, to send paint, books, scrapbooks, and other material for children's meetings, how He laid it on others to send gifts and treats to give out for Christmas. Some sent Bibles and Testaments for careful distribution, books for our library, our clothing, shoes, furniture and many other things. We could tell how those who fought us at first in our charge became our friends, how our folk sacrificed and gave to missions, how we have grieved with those who were bearing great sorrow and how God comforted their hearts. Surely it has paid us a hundredfold in joy, peace, and happiness for minding God. We prayed for milk goats; we had them almost before we realized it. We have felt for some time that the Lord wanted us to do more toward our support, so we are planning to raise chickens. We are trusting God to take care of that expense. Our days and weeks are very full, but God has helped us to be methodical and systematic with our duties. We have 'Method-ist' blood flowing in our veins.

"Once I was lost in the woods. My sense of direction left me, my flashlight (of little value on long trips) went out, and I was left in the dark—no moon, and heavy clouds covered the stars. I tried to guess my position by listening to distant trains, but they were too far off. I called but was out of hearing of any person. I prayed and kept note of position where I first realized I was lost. I began to feel carefully as I stepped for that narrow, hard-packed line that I knew was the path. Autumn leaves had covered it, but the Lord helped, and I soon found it.

"Friday night, June 14, 1940, about 10:30 I left for a doctor. The nurse stayed with my wife. The nearest phone was at the station four miles distant. I made it in thirty minutes. To my relief the boat was on my side of the river. After some difficulty I roused the station agent, and she went to the railroad phone. The dispatcher was very accommodating but relayed the message to us that the doctor's son-in-law was seriously ill and he could not come—the doctor we had engaged. My dismay could not be expressed. I then asked if he would mind calling another doctor. The station agent kindly suggested that going after one might have more force to it than sending. I went to a near-by house and succeeded in rousing a young man I knew. We started off to Beattyville, the county seat of Lee County. He barely had enough gasoline to get to a station, but we purchased some and were in Beattyville around midnight. No help there. We started to Booneville, county seat of Wolfe County. Still we had no success. We started off again and in Jackson, county seat of Breathitt County, we located a doctor who agreed to come. We started back. We brought the car within a mile of home—the nearest we could get. There was still the river to contend with. This boat landing was closer than the one I crossed going, but as might have been expected the boat was on the opposite side. The river was past fording, so I knew I couldn't wade across. After a few minutes of fruitless calling, I went up the river a short distance, found a place that looked more shallow, took off part of my clothes, held them above my head and struck out. Fortunately, the water was only to my chest, and I did not have to swim and get my clothes wet. I put on my clothes, located the boat, and paddled across to get the doctor. About five-thirty A. M. we stepped on our porch. I was muddy and barefooted, carrying my shoes in one hand, and the doctor's bag in the other. There I was informed by Miss Yoss, the nurse from Mt. Carmel, that I had a son three hours old, but the doctor's attention was needed, and after a brief visit he left. We named this boy John Wesley. I collected my scattered senses and gave thanks from the depths of my heart to the God who doeth all things well.

"Our new location at Index, Ky., is more convenient; thus, we are not so handicapped, as we are on a highway with a phone just across the road. We have been here about a month. Our station is not important; as long as we are engaged in a spiritual ministry, we are happy. Handicaps teach us to be more patient and to appreciate conveniences when we do get them."

With workers coming from so many states and denominations, the work could not have been maintained except for the Holy Ghost in sanctifying power in the hearts and lives of the workers and the converts. Unless the Lord had founded and continued the Kentucky Mountain Holiness Association, Lela G. McConnell and her corps of co-laborers would have failed. Giving ourselves unreservedly to the preaching and teaching of the full gospel, has been the entire secret of our success.

If ever the time comes when the Kentucky Mountain Holiness Association gradually loses its burning zeal for holiness of heart and life, the strenuous, practical, self-sacrificing toil, the simple faith and willingness to be poor, it will become miserable and useless. Also if clamoring for leadership and the desire to become popular and big take the place of tender love for each other, the time of our downfall will soon come.

Eighteen years have elapsed since we began; yet to the glory of God we can truthfully say that the Association was never more closely knit together in the bonds of rich fellowship. A deep, spiritual ministry pervades each school and station. God's rich grace has sufficed for every time of hardship and severe testing. Beginnings have their incentive, but the long stretch of years is the greatest test. The cleanness of the work and trueness of the Association to holiness has brought great satisfaction to my heart.

Acts 19-17, With Paul we can say, "And the name of the Lord Jesus was magnified."

CHAPTER VII

Remarkable Answers To Prayer

Through the years we have been enabled to prove the faithfulness of the Covenant Keeping God in supplying every need in answer to prayer.

"In everything by prayer and supplication with thanksgiving let your requests be made known unto God. And the peace of God, which passeth all understanding, shall keep your hearts and minds through Christ Jesus." Just to be able to trust God fully for everything does not come to us over night. No, the Lord cannot trust us with any more than he sees we deserve or have the faith that asks from entirely unselfish motives. It is rich how the Lord keeps our hearts and minds peaceful in Him in a work of faith.

Paul rejoiced at the liberality of the Philippians and wrote back to them, "But my God shall supply all your need according to his riches in glory by Christ Jesus." Riches of His grace and love and care are far greater than money.

God has called many of us to labor for Him here for life. We work as hard as we can; we have enough to eat and enough to wear and a place to sleep. What more is life than this? Our rewards in spiritual blessings and souls far outweigh the temporal things of earth. "Godliness with contentment is great gain."

One of our precious mountain girls who came to us at the age of eighteen has been a real prayer warrior these twelve years. Her faith in answer to victorious obedience is given briefly in the following lines:

"When I want help and comfort I don't go to Jonah, for he failed God one time and never did get fixed up just right as I thought he ought to. But I do go to Daniel, for the Word says that 'Daniel purposed in his heart that he would not defile himself with the portion of the king's meat, nor with the wine which he drank,' etc. Daniel was a strong character, and he was going through with God in spite of the king and everything. It tickled me how the old king, who wanted to please the people, went and called into the lion's den, 'O Daniel, servant of the living God, is thy God whom thou servest continually, able to deliver thee from the lions?" Daniel was able to answer with strong assurances, "O King, live forever, my God hath sent His angel and has shut the lions' mouths that they have not hurt me.' I just wonder how the old weak king felt along about that time. I also wonder how a disobedient, weak, erring one feels when he looks into the face of persecution, ill-will, calamities, and what not, and sees God's grace continually sufficient for those who are trying to do 'whatsoever he saith' unto them.

"Now, when we've got the purpose in our hearts and God has helped us to overcome these things, there are still other testings. Maybe God has called you to go out into some faith work. Folks will say, 'You'll starve to death,' 'You'll get killed,' and all sorts of things. People sometimes say to me, 'How do you live? Don't you get any salary? Looks as though you'd have to have somebody back of you.' Well, we do have Somebody back of us. If I depended on some of you, you might fail me, but if I depend upon Jesus He never fails. He owns everything, and all He has belongs to us if we can just get hold of it.

"When I went out in station work, Miss McConnell told us not to go out and starve; if we needed anything, to write in for it. But I made up my mind that if one person could trust the Lord for everything I could, too. Three of us girls went to a station together. All of us were as poor as could be and hadn't a bit of money. After a time, our food was getting low. We were praying for money, each one of us. On Thursday the supply was getting more scanty and no food nor money coming in. We were praying in family prayer, our private devotions, special prayer, and every kind of prayer we knew to pray. Friday passed. no money and no food came in. We were stretching our meager amount as far as it would go. On Monday two of us girls got a letter from a nurse in Lexington. She enclosed a check for $5.00 to be divided between the two of us, and we were so happy to share with the other also. I don't want anybody to feel sorry for me over that experience. I can see many reasons for it. That verse, 'What I do thou knowest not now, but thou shalt know hereafter,' has been a great blessing to me. Did our faith fail? No. Did God fail? No! No! This girl went ahead to say in her letter that she felt definitely impressed on Thursday to send us some money. That's the day we were praying every kind of prayer we knew of. *God answers prayer*, and I've never starved to death once.

"If we obey God we'll have a good enough house

to live in, enough to eat, enough to wear, and plenty
of friends to take us in their cars. We'll have lots of
good Christians to pray for us and all the peace and
joy our little hearts can hold.

"Don't be afraid to go out into any service to which
God calls you. He is first, and we're following closely
behind Him. All things must first come to Him before
they reach us. He gives grace and glory. He answers
prayer. He never fails. He carries the heaviest end
of the load always. 'Whatsoever he saith unto you,
do it.' And as you do it, don't be afraid to hide behind the name of Jesus."

It is no small thing that God has fulfilled His promises to us. It is also a great cause of encouragement.

"Seek ye first the kingdom of God and his righteousness; and all these things shall be added unto you."

We had just established the Kentucky Mountain
Bible Institute. There was an old gas well about a mile
and a half up the creek that was filled with water and
had caved in. We leased the well and contracted with
a man from West Liberty, Ky., to come and clean out
the well. He moved the rig on the site and began bail-
ing out the water and the sand. After he had worked
for a numbr of days, he began to tell us that there was
no gas there and we might as well stop the work. By
this time the weather was getting quite cold and we
had no means to heat or light the Bible School whatsoever. Up to this time we had used coal oil stoves to
cook with and oil lamps for light. We said, "We know
there is gas there. God has assured us of that." He
said, "I have been in this business for many years and

I know the gas has all gone from the well." Mr. Swauger, who was helping him, would pray and ask him to work a little longer. The contractor was about to quit the job and go home. We had a fast prayer meeting at the Bible School. The Lord reassured us that we were to have gas out of this well. Prayer of this kind was all new to the driller and it was making a great impression on him. Mr. Swauger in his distress knelt down near the well and prayed and came back and said to the driller, "Let's go down with the bailer just once more." To please Mr. Swauger he started the motor and down 1500 feet the 20-foot bailer went to the bottom of the well. As he brought it up they could smell gas and in just a few seconds there was a noise like an explosion, a mighty flow of gas. The men stood back lest they would get hurt. Mr. Swauger praised the Lord and immediately sent a runner down the creek to the School with the good news. What a time of rejoicing we did have. We gave God all the praise for He alone did it. The gas has supplied our Bible School since that time for all cooking, heating, and lighting purposes.

At the Mt. Carmel School we were given a gas well that was plugged up. A number of years before our school was built some oil company had leased the land in certain localities all through Breathitt County prospecting for oil. They had drilled down nearly 1500 feet in this well, but no oil. However, there was a good flow of gas. The folk in the neighborhood did not want it. They said they had no use for gas and were afraid of it. These oil well men filled the hole up with iron tools, chestnut saplings, and stones so as to prevent the gas from ecscaping. They did not succeed entirely however, and so a constant flow of gas was filling the air. It had to be lighted in order to keep folk who lived near it from getting sick. For miles around you could see the light of this well at night when the gas was burning. We harnessed all of it and piped it to the school. It heated the boys' dormitory and was enough for the cooking arrangements. After the school grew larger and we had almost double the number of rooms to heat when we enlarged our plant, there was not enough gas. We decided to clean out the well. Mr. Guy Meabon, a good sanctified man from Huntington, W. Va., volunteered to come and do it free. Brother Meabon has given us many lifts with our gas wells at both boarding schools. The Lord bless and reward him for all of these great kindnesses. We were so thankful, for this was a very definite answer to prayer. They had a great deal of trouble getting through the things which the oil well men had plugged it with. The tools would get hung in the well or the line would break. One day the great long stem was stuck far down in the well. They worked for three days and often into the night to get it loose. Mr. Meabon and Mrs. Swauger and I had a season of prayer. This time without any strain even on the line, the heavy two ton tool came slowly out of the well. The man working at the engine said, "The line is broken; there does not seem to be any load on it at all." No doubt the Lord, instead of the line, was pulling it up. A great shout of praise to God ascended when the big

tool came out at the top of the well. Once more our
faithful God saw our helplessness and distress and did
for us the impossible. We praised God from the bottom of our hearts and gave Him all the glory. I believe the Lord loves to have us prove Him in this way.

Two men got into an argument over a small bill of
less than $5.00 for some corn. They began to fight.
One of them was killed. While he was dying his little
daughter kept telling him, "Father, I'll kill the man
that shot you." Some time after the funeral she went
to the jail well armed in order to carry out her promise to her father. She was not permitted to see the
prisoner. A few days later the man was mobbed by
a masked crowd that broke into the county jail.. They
took him up the highway a few miles and put thirteen
bullets in him, leaving him for dead. In the morning
some men passing by heard his groans and took him to
the hospital where he died in a few days. The trial
came off later in the year. Some folk declared there
would be wholesale murder in the county such as folk
had never seen. It had gotten into politics and had
divided the people in such a manner that it was talked
about throughout the county. Some of our students
had friends on both sides of the issue. The tension
ran high. Again and again one of our Sophomore
girls, a native of Breathitt County and who knew the
case so well through hearing her father discuss it,
would request prayer in our Wednesday night prayer
meetings for God to undertake in this fearful situation. This young woman was mighty in prayer. I can
hear her yet pleading with the Lord to take out the

hatred and subdue and help those on both sides. Many of us would lift while she prayed. Often also in our faculty prayer meetings God would burden us for it. We have no doubt that the Lord undertook. As far as we know not a person in either family or their kinsfolk have been killed since that time. God's power is unlimited. "The effectual fervent prayer of the righteous man availeth much." Like Moses when he prayed for the people, the Lord answered him; and the Lord heard the prayer of this young woman for the people of her county and answered her.

The young people of the mountains bear soul burden in a remarkable way. A well established young woman in the Senior class was under the burden for another student who had trifled so long with God. She professed to get saved a number of times, but there were no evidences in her life She would rush to the altar in our revival meetings time and again. In a few minutes she would get up and testify that the Lord had forgiven her sins. Finally, one of the faculty felt it was time to expose such action in order to help other students who were seeking. She did not like this. After the service was dismissed and the students were going to their rooms, this Senior girl got hold of God and walked the floor, crying unto the Lord to save the girl who was trifling with God. The unsaved girl came running into the office and fell on her knees and begged us to pray for her, this time with real repentance. She made much confession and restitution back in her home and gave up all sin. She kept on seeking for two days. Finally, God came in saving grace, and oh, the glory and blessing that she received from the Lord. In the same revival she sought the Lord and He sanctified her. For years her life and testimony were most precious. The Lord had not put that soul burden on the Senior girl to mock her. No, she held on, and the Holy Ghost used it to cause the unsaved one to yield fully to God.

On another similar occasion Miss Day was overwhelmed in soul agony for a Senior student. The girl rushed to the altar and prayed through. This young woman felt led to give her testimony after she had given her oration on Commencement day. Her father and the audience wept as she gave her experience in detail of the Lord's dealings with her.

Sometimes these special burdens come upon us for students. A young man was saved in the same revival. One of the faculty held on to God for his soul until he fell at his seat and cried for mercy. Later he testified about it at Asbury College.

All of our revivals are promoted by the workers and the converts fasting and praying. A man, seventy-five years old, who had sought the Lord so often, said to me, "I can't get saved; I'm too ignorant." We assured him that he could. One of our evangelists, Miss Archer, and her singer, Miss Violet Person, who has done such excellent work for years in our Association and teaching in the High School and Bible School, were conducting a revival on his creek the fall of 1941. He gave up all sins; asked his wife in all humility to forgive him for the way he had treated her, and dug down until he struck the rock. His tobacco went and all. The Lord met him in saving power. His wife helped him in the home to consecrate step by step until all was on the altar and the fire fell and sanctified him wholly.

A note of $500 was coming due. The assurance came after much praying and believing God. The day came, but no money to pay the $500. We could not understand it. God had not failed us we knew. I went to the bank and told them that the Lord had heard our prayers, but we did not have the money then. A few months later I had an opportunity to speak at a convention in Indianapolis, Ind., for about ten minutes. I noticed an elderly man in the audience weeping much as I told them of the blessings of the Lord upon our work and souls finding God. At the close of the service he rushed to me and said, "Little sister, who are you?" He had never seen me before. After he learned my name he told me that he had read in the *Heart and Life Bulletin*, a paper published by the Chicago Evangelistic Institute, an article some time ago about the work of the Kentucky Mountains that had my name signed to it. He laid the paper down and said to his wife, "I must send that sister $500." That was the time we felt the assurance of the money for our note. He said, "Here it is now." I rushed home from the convention and into our bank in Jackson and paid the note. Sometimes the enemy gets in and hinders, but God overrules when our faith fails not.

Brother Warren C. McIntire was scheduled to be our camp meeting evangelist. He came one week early to help in a revival in one of the out-stations. He preached to a crowded house each night. A young man with two guns and partly intoxicated had crowded half way up to the front of the schoolhouse. Brother McIntire in his message was saying, "Young man, take back that bridle or that stirrup you stole," and went on to list other things. The young man with guns deliberately laid one on the floor and with the other one pointed at the evangelist, and said, "Preacher, you say that again and I'll shoot you." Brother McIntire went right on preaching as though nothing had happened. He was staying in a near by home. He felt strangely, but definitely, led not to take the usual little path to the place that night. He crept up through the woods in a round-about way. The next day he learned that the young man was hiding in ambush to pick him off. The Lord takes care of his own.

The National Association of Local Preachers met in Washington, D. C., in November, 1926. Our debts were many and folk were pressing us for money. We felt from the beginning that the Lord wanted us to trust Him fully and not go around and ask folk for money. I said, "Well, I'm a member of the National Association of Local Preachers and I'll just go and ask them at the convention for about $15,000 which would help us with the pressing needs." I had often attended these conventions and knew that many of the members were big business men with lots of money. They asked me to speak and gave me a whole half hour to talk about the work. The devil said, "Now is your chance to ask this convention for $15,000." Well, to the hurt of my soul I did, but God surely stepped in

and defeated the enemy's plan because the folk gave
me just $2.50, and I have been praising God ever since
that it wasn't any more. If they had given me a lot
of money, the lovely plan of God for our whole trust
in Him would have been upset and we would have gotten into all kinds of difficulties. On the train coming
home I was praying and the Lord opened my eyes to it
all and I resolved by God's grace that we would follow
His plan for us in this phase of the work. That night
I told the faculty and they said they all felt the same
about it. The blessing of the Lord melted our souls
afresh as we drove one more stake down for God and
holiness and to keep in His will. These temptations
to compromise along financial lines will come upon us
so subtlely unless we keep well prayed up. Our faith
was often tested, we felt, to the breaking point, but
the rich growth in grace came constantly as we held
firm under the guiding and comforting hand of our
Heavenly Father. I found it very easy to trust God
for my own needs, but it was an entirely different
proposition to have faith for large food bills, gas wells,
cars, new churches and parsonages and new dormitories that cost tens of thousands of dollars.

My sister wrote me that one of our cousins was
very ill and could not recover. I said to the faculty,
"Let's pray that God will lay it on her heart to give us
$500 for the spread of holiness in the mountains." We
met in the chapel and prayed for some time. As so
often happened, the Lord let us understand that He
would attend to it. We left it entirely in His hands,
not praying any more about it. She lived about six

weeks. I saw the nurse the following summer. She said, "Your cousin, a few weeks before she died talked about you a lot. She even had us get a lawyer to change her will and give you $500 extra above the other eighteen first cousins. She was so happy over it. And when that was off her mind she rested much better." No doubt God had a double purpose in it all —to help her spiritually by investing some money in our vital soul-saving work, as well as to strengthen our faith in Him. My check was $1362.45. I bought a dress for $4.00 and a pair of shoes for $3.00 which I needed very badly, and gave all the rest to the work of the Lord and felt powerfully blest. Some folk criticised me for this and said, "What will happen if you get sick, and what are you going to do when you get old?" I said, "The Lord has all of that planned for me if I obey Him fully and keep in the center of His will.' Psalm 84:11. "The Lord God is a sun and shield; the Lord will give grace and glory; no good thing will he withhold from them that walk uprightly." This rich promise has been vindicated in my behalf often. I thank God that He has seen me through two hospital experiences and kept me clothed through these now nearly full eighteen years of labor in the mountains. I handle all the money that comes in and thus could be free to use it for my personal needs, but I have never been tempted to do it. I live like all the dear teachers and pastors who are full of devotion and sacrifice in order that the Lord be magnified in the mountains Often money is labeled, 'personal to Miss McConnell,' I rarely use it. All I have needed in cash through these years is less than $1,000 for my own personal needs. Dear friends have sent me clothing and donated medical care, etc. My faith no doubt would fall many times if I spent any money unnecessarily on myself. Furthermore, how could I pray money out of other people's bank account if I had one of my own?

Already the Lord has begun to take care and provide for me as I get older. The faculty got it on their hearts to ask the Lord to provide a place where I could rest better and live separate from the dormitories. They felt the time had come, when for the sake of the Association, with so many more responsibilities, I needed to conserve my strength. I tried to discourage them in this move. They prayed. A very kind friend sent in $1,000 designating the check for Miss McConnel's Cottage. Later when the secretary wrote and thanked him she said, "Mr. Swauger and I have closely estimated a little home for Miss McConnell. (The design they got from the *Better Homes and Garden Magazine*). It will cost $1800." God touched his heart so that he sent the $800 also. This very kind friend has often helped us. Again and again he would write from the Pacific Coast and say, "Let me know your needs," which we very seldom did.

After the foundation was built for the cottage the "flash flood" came. We stopped the work to take care of the rebuilding of the Kentucky Mountain Bible Institute. I wanted to write the donor and ask him to let me use the cottage money for the many immediate needs after the flood. The faculty said, "No." Many times they look after me about such matters. All are so good and solicitous of my welfare. I thank the Lord for sending me such marvelous true and tried, capable, sanctified men and women of the Mt. Carmel and Kentucky Mountain Bible Institute faculties. At Mt. Carmel the present faculty are: Mr. and Mrs. R. L. Swauger, Genelle Day, Mary Swartout, Elma Reed, Mr. and Mrs. Karl Paulo, Lorene Clayton, Edith Morgan, and George Thomas. The faculty at the Kentucky Mountain Bible Institute are: Martha L. Archer, Mrs H. P. Myers, Mildred Drake, Celia Gibson, Mr. and Mrs. Wilfred Fisher, Miriam Gregory and Mrs. Ida Weber. All but four of these eighteen have felt God's call to spend their lives in the work. Their coming has been a most remarable answer to prayer. They represent twelve states (Oregon has the majority) and five denominations. Fourteen of these are Methodists.

The faithful group of pastors are also with us in direct answer to prayer. It is marvelous how God has picked them up from so many parts of the United States and from so many denominations. The present members of the Conference whom God has laid His hands on for their life ministry in the Kentucky Mountain Holiness Association are: Madge Carter, Mary Paulo, Mr. and Mrs. Louis Bouck, Mr. and Mrs. Forrest Cox, Mattie White, Eunice Taulbee, Mr. and Mrs. Carl Faulkner, Eunice Kirk, Lena Perry, Olive Perry, Mr. and Mrs. Glen Des Jardins, Geleah Mollenkopf, Sybil Wilburn, Fay Holman, Mr. and Mrs. Eddie Lockwood, Jean Sitter, Ruth Hahn, Irene Baird, Paul Major, Violet Person, Helen Ann Halushchak.

The group of young people who are still in our
schools or away to get further training, but who are
settled in their calls to the mountains, are a great joy
to our hearts. We give them seven years of training
in our schools. After they have finished the years of
training in the Kentucky Mountain Bible Institute, we
then appoint them assistant pastors. With two years
of close supervision in the pastorate, if they prove
themselves, we then ordain them and appoint them to
the pastorate to spread scriptural holiness throughout
the mountains in our stations. With these nine years
of preparation they feel that they are settled to trust
the Lord in every place and help to lift the burdens for
the advancement of God's kingdom along with those
who are older. The present list is: Dorothy Spencer,
Richard Stauffer, Mabel Wilson, Albert Landrum,
Lockeye Carlisle, Mr. and Mrs. Marvin Wheeler, Edith
Vandewarker, Edith Lockard, and Teressa Brayton.
We pray that none of these young people will fail God,
and that through the coming years a greater number
will be called to labor for souls here along the creeks
and up the hollows where over one half million people
are in Eastern Kentucky waiting yet for the full gospel.

Later the cottage was finished and I moved into it
September, 1940. It is very nice and comfortable.
Most of the furniture was donated. The station workers and the faculties of the two schools gave me lovely
showers. Mrs. Elizabeth Jordan, of Atlantic City,
gave much of the furniture and $50.00 to get it here.

The main building at Mt. Carmel is heated by steam. It takes about ninety tons of coal each year to run the furnace. At the end of the fifteenth year of hard usage with soft coal one section of the boiler had a crack in it. This we fixed with boiler cement. Two years later the same thing happened with the back section of the boiler. We tried the cement again, but it just would not work because the crack was too large We sent for an agent to come and look it over. He advised an entirely new boiler. He said that ours had lasted longer than the average with this kind of coal. What were we to do? Trust the Lord in this emergency like we had done many times. We explained to the agent that we did not have any money to pay on it now. He then wrote to the company in Huntington, W. Va. They said, "We will ship the furnace at once; we have heard of the faith of these people." In five days the furnace arrived. It weighed 4200 pounds. Our professors and boys carried it across the swinging bridge where we loaded it in our old campus truck, which we made out of the 1926 Dodge, and hauled it up the Blue Bird Trail. The men and boys on the campus installed it and had it working fine in a few days. Our men are very capable and versatile and then too, they have lots of sense and salvation and that is what it takes to be a missionary anywhere. In a very short time we paid $400 on it and the balance a little later. God is faithful.

We have been getting our coal from a farmer near by for sixteen years. His health gave out. He offered to sell us the coal mine which is about a mile from our campus. We prayed about it and felt led to take it. At the same time we began to feel uneasy about this same farmer planning to clear off the land around our swinging bridge. We knew if all the big trees were taken off, erosion would take place and thus endanger the bridge. The "dead men" might be pulled up and this would of course cause the cables to give way and the bridge would fall. We asked him to sell us the woodland on the river bank. He charged us $500 for the 10.7 acres of woodland and 3:5 acres of coal in the mine. We figured up the coal—a small vein and three and a half acres of it. By burning one hundred tons a year, it will last us over a hundred years. The money was due November 1st because the farmer had to meet the last payment to the Federal Land Bank at Louisville at that time, to finish paying for his entire farm. This time the Lord gave us such a good surprise and arranged for the money ahead of time. In the mail one day a letter came from an attorney in East Liverpool, Ohio. It read like this: "Mrs. ——————— has willed you $500. The money will be coming to you in about thirty days. Of course if you don't need this money, we will not force it on you." At once we praised the Lord and wrote the lawyer just what God had done in answering prayer for the money coming due so soon. The Lord has truly convinced the people in the bank and the business men with whom we deal constantly, that He is faithful to all those who put their trust in Him. Our job is to keep the wheels of faith unclogged. Beloved, "If our hearts condemn us not, then have we confidence toward God. For if our heart condemn us God is greater than our heart, and knoweth all things."

A young man of twenty summers had rejected God many times. He was now a Junior. God visited him by giving him a vision of dropping into hell. No revival was on. He came running to the altar without an invitation for seekers. He confessed his sins quickly. God came nearer and nearer. All the students were weeping. He deliberately stood up and confessed to the entire student body and faculty how he sinned against God and the school. His intelligent, Scriptural, seeking was soon rewarded. God spoke peace to his troubled soul. He is now in the army on the Pacific Coast. He wrote me this month (March, 1942) that the Lord was in his heart in saving grace and in sanctifying power and that he found God's grace sufficient. He said, "The men and officers respect my religion." I wrote him a letter of encouragement. These rewards pile up year after year. "The mountains shall be thine; and the outgoings of it shall be thine." Josh. 17:18.

Numbers 9:23, "At the commandment of the Lord they rested in the tents, and at the commandment of the Lord they journeyed; they kept the charge of the Lord, at the commandment of the Lord by the hand of Moses." At different times in the history of our work we have felt the "cloud lifting" which meant, like the Israelites, we were to move on.

Many of our workers have been those whom God had called to be foreign missionaries. They had come to help us before getting out to the field where God

had called them. Then too, in a few years after our
schools were established, a number of our students felt
the call of God to go across the waters. It was laid
upon our hearts almost simultaneously that we must
do something to encourage and help them. Miss Alice
Day, who has been in Africa six years now, was with
us teaching at Mt. Carmel for five years. Miss Day
really belongs to me. In the early days of my evangelistic work I found her in a small village in Eastern
Pennsylvania. I encouraged and helped her through
the years to answer the call of God upon her life. I
have talked to a few folk who have contacted her on
their world tours. They tell me that God's rich sanctifying grace upon her is making her a marked blessing among the Kipsigis in South Africa. At the
Christmas Conference in 1932, Miss Day brought up
the subject of organizing a foreign missionary prayer
band at Mt. Carmel. Immediately we all felt God was
moving us on in that direction. She organized the
band. Soon the out-stations took it up and now we
have seventeen Prayer Bands in our Association. They
are under the National Holiness Missionary Society
whose headquarters is in Chicago. The president is
Dr. G. Arnold Hodgin and the secretary is Rev. George
Warner. Our work also has auxiliary relationship
with the National Holiness Association, an interdenominational organization for the promotion of Scriptural holiness, which was organized seventy-eight
years ago by three Methodist preachers in Philadelphia. Dr. C. W. Butler of John Fletcher College, has
been the president for the last fourteen years.

Many missionaries have gone to foreign fields after being with us for a few years. They write back their deep gratitude for the training and blessing in our home field in this Interdenominational work of faith. The sacrificial giving of our mountain people touches our hearts. They love to give and pray for the people in heathen lands. Last year our Prayer Bands and Sunday Schools gave $478 to foreign missions. Miss Gertrude Shryock, R. N., who was our school nurse and also one of our high school teachers, is now in Africa. The Lord used her greatly in promoting our Prayer Band work. Miss Frances Beard, another Asbury College graduate, had charge of the Kentucky State Prayer Bands while she was teaching in our high school and Bible School. On account of the war she could not go to Africa. She is now doing very effective service for God in winning souls in Central America while she is waiting to get to the field of Africa where God called her some years ago.

A few years ago we were in desperate need. We had been praying for some time for God to lift these burdens. In our praying we said, "O Lord, if the people in America won't answer our cries please touch hearts around the world. In less than two weeks $62 came to us from Africa. Isa. 65:24, "And it shall come to pass that before they call, I will answer; and while they are yet speaking, I will hear."

In our revivals we fast and pray much. We find it harder to pray a revival down than to pray in money. The pastor will send out word all over the Association to have folk in the other stations and in the schools to pray for their revival. Thus a volume of prayer is ascending for God to handle all the tactics of the devil and for the outpouring of the Holy Ghost upon the services. Folk whom God sees are hungry and ripe are reached in each meeting. Others are getting more light so that probably in the next meeting they will seek and find God. Rarely do we have a great number to pray through in our revivals in the stations, but God does give us splendid hand-picked fruit. The battle against holiness is always raging. Fearlessly we go right on preaching the Word and our converts one by one see the light and come through good into this marvelous "second rest." Their sanctified hearts tell mightily toward convincing their neighbors and kinsfolk about the realities of salvation full and free. Beloved, these rewards make up for all else. Our group of co-laborers with God are supremely happy. It does not take a salary to make folk enjoy life. "I am come that they might have life and that they might have it more abundantly." It is this more abundant life of full salvation that gives gracious power and victory over the world, the flesh, and the devil.

For six years beginning 1927, Mr. and Mrs. W. B. Weaver helped us in the Annual Holiness Camp Meeting. Brother Weaver was a member of the Detroit Conference for nearly fifty years. God made him a great factor in our camp. His ministry was very helpful. He was also a member of our Board of Trustees. In January, 1935, the Lord took him Home to be with Him. Since then Mrs. Weaver has been coming to sew for us each spring and fall. Her godly life and seasoned advice has given us many lifts. Always we look forward to her coming.

After the Camp closed one year the two evangelists, Brother Weaver and Rev. Charles Jacobs, who was also a Methodist from the Detroit Conference, were asked to go to Devil's Creek and baptize a number of our converts who lived along that creek. Neither of the preachers ever traveled over roads like these. However, we came to the end of the road. The community folk had dammed up Devil's Creek to baptize the saints of God in and there we stood on the bank while the Lord witnessed to our hearts of His pleasure as Brother Weaver immersed the people. We have had many such services all over the various districts of our Kentucky Mountain Holiness Association.

I must relate to you one or two more very remarkable answers to prayer. We were having our all-day meeting at one of the out appointments. Brother Joseph H. Smith was with us for five days and thus these all-day meetings were planned ahead of time. At this time also Brother Smith was the speaker at our June Conference which is held for two days each year at the Headquarters of the Association. Brother R. L. Swauger took a load of us in the car with Brother Smith. The roads had not dried up from the spring rains. In bouncing over the deep ruts and in plowing through the mud, the old car got something wrong with it. We had started early knowing the condition of the trail. However, after so long a time when the car would not start, some of us walked on to the church to begin the service. There were many mules hitched around so we asked one of the boys, who had been a student at Mt. Carmel that year, if he wouldn't take his mule and go back after Brother Smith. When the boy came riding up to the car he said to Mr. Swauger, "They sent me with this mule for Brother Smith to ride on." Brother Smith said to the boy, "I wouldn't know what to do with the mule and I don't know what the mule would do with me." The young man came back without our speaker. Mr. Swauger worked while he prayed. He said, "Brother Smith, I've done all I know to do." Just then he leaned over the steering wheel and called on the Lord again. Brother Smith's heart was touched. Without doing another thing, Mr. Swauger tried to start the car and this time, in direct answer to prayer, the Lord Himself made it go. How thankful was that waiting crowd to hear the car come splashing up the creek and on to the ground where the praise service had been going on for some time. Brother Smith told his life story and the people hung on his words. His ministry was a benediction to all of us.

It was nearly midnight. We had prayed many times. The crowd had all gone home. Yet this one lone seeker would not give up. He wanted God. He said he had recently planned to kill a man in the Chenowee tunnel. We held on in faith. He would cry and pray as only a boy nineteen years old can. We noticed that he kept his hand under his coat all the time. All of a sudden he raised up and said, "I can't give her up! I can't give her up!" We thought it was some young woman of course. No, he finally drew his arm from under his coat and in his hand was a 38 Smith-Wesson. He laid it on the altar. The Lord began to come on the scene and our hearts felt a mighty lift. He still prayed on. He said, "I'll have to give that up too." It was his tobacco. After a very few minutes of praying and asking the Lord to save him, he stood up and said, "The Lord saves me." He did not need to tell us. The light of heaven was in his face and the joy of it was felt by the evangelist and the workers. No case is too hard for the Lord.

Now we have Miss Miriam Gregory, one of the music teachers at Kentucky Mountain Bible Institute, as state president of the Prayer Bands. Her whole heart and soul is in the work here as she looks forward to China after the war is over.

These vital interests connect us up with many countries and make us a world institution. Forty-two foreign missionaries have spoken in our chapel the last fourteen years and also visited many of the stations. We feel that God has wonderfully favored this holiness center. Missionary Day at our annual camp meeting is always a great feast to our souls. Our station people begin to plan a way to come on that day as soon as the camp begins and the day is announced. One man walked sixteen miles to get here. There is a charm and a grandeur about this old gospel that surmounts all difficulties and knows no barriers. We praise the Lord that He has given us a share in it. Not only the mountains shall be thine, but also some trophies around the world. Souls are the same everywhere. A world vision brings us so into the presence of God that we want to proclaim to dying men everywhere the thunderings of Sinai, the joys of Calvary, and the comforts of Pentecost.

CHAPTER VIII

Helpful Advice To Christians—Especially To Christian Workers

I was traveling through New England visiting the various Holiness Camp Meetings during the worst of the depression days when I received such an encouraging letter from one of our evangelists back in the mountains. I answered it thus: "Your letter did me a lot of good. I feel that God is giving us all a better grip on the Mountain people and situations. I praise God for the revivals. I do believe that God can use our local workers as much as the big evangelists because they understand the people so well. Let us hold all of our precious workers to a high standard and then they will either get in or get out. Let us honor the Holy Ghost in all things and He will add a dignity and a depth and a power to our workers and the work that will tell mightily for souls and the Kingdom of God.

"The Adirondack Mountains and the Lakes every-where are all so beautiful; tourists by the thousands here; no signs of depression. I was talking to a lady on this train. She said her niece had just spent $85,000 to make their home more beautiful. Oh, the folly of it all and we need money so much for our extreme needs. "They sent me with this mule for Brother Smith to get to the next place. God surely has money for us some place. We will keep on trusting Him fully."

I have quoted the above paragraphs from a letter, which I just now unearthed among other things in the files of the office, in order to emphasize two points in it. First—holding our pastors and teachers to a standard spiritually that is sane, sensible, and Scriptural. Second—to hold steady as Christian workers amidst hard financial pulls and not compromise. With the finances for the work we have nothing to do, but with God we have everything to do. The big problems of the Christian's life are summed up in three phases; spiritual, temporal and social. Be open and downright honest in public and in private in holiness of heart and life and God's work will succeed; no compromise between profession and practice.

The multiplied good promises in God's word are all for us if we will meet the conditions. The Lord often permits our faith to be tested in order to deepen us in the divine walk and warfare. Nowhere does He promise us an easy time. Our all-wise God knew just how to arrange things in order that we may enjoy to the fullest extent the rich spiritual benefits of Calvary ourselves and thus be fitted to help others. The highest, deepest and grandest things that come to us on this earth are the spiritual values. While we do not pay in temporal values to secure salvation, yet there is a price to pay in a far deeper sense. The Christians who are supremely happy and enjoying salvation today, as in all ages, have paid the price in making their wrongs right and their crooked places straight by confessing their sins to God and to man; that is, whatever the Lord shows them. Then by faith they can say, "Therefore being justified by faith, we have peace with God through our Lord Jesus Christ." This peace with

God has no substitute. All our sins are under the blood.
Praise God—"There is a fountain filled with blood,
Drawn from Immanuel's veins, And sinners plunged
beneath that flood; Lose all their guilty stains." Having driven this stake down, then go on into the Canaan
Land Experience of Holiness. This too, beloved, has a
price which is Romans 12:1, 2—presenting ourselves
to the Lord completely willingly and voluntarily. It is
laying all on the altar, which is Jesus. Take my life,
my moments, my hands, my feet, my voice, my silver,
my intellect, my will, my heart, my love, and myself.
With this consecration Jesus will sanctify you wholly.
You can then prove what is that good and acceptable,
and perfect will of God. The blood of Jesus has cleansed out all carnality and your heart is clean. You now
know the double cure. "Be of sin the double cure, Save
from wrath and make me pure." "And the peace of
God which passeth all understanding shall keep your
hearts and minds through Christ Jesus."

As long as we keep these two stakes driven down
we are in a position to grow in grace and to fulfill
God's plan for our lives. We will constantly be a con-
structive force for good and the advancement of God's
glorious Kingdom. We will be laying up treasures in
Heaven. In spite of the fact that, since Adam's fall,
we have had nearly six thousand years of infirmity
piled upon us, we can live a victorious life through Jesus over the world, the flesh, and the devil. When the
Lord saves us, the love of the world is all gone. 1 John
2:15, "If any man love the world the love of the Father
is not in him." 1 John 5:4. For "whosoever is born

of God overcometh the world." James says we are to
keep ourselves unspotted from the world. When the
Lord cleanses our hearts then we have victory over the
flesh (the Greek word for flesh here is carnality.) Before we are saved or sanctified the works of the flesh
are manifested as listed in Gal. 5:19, 20 and 21, and
they which do such things says Paul, "shall not inherit
the kingdom of God." On the other hand, after the
Lord saves us and then sanctifies us, we have the fruit
of the Spirit listed in Gal. 5:22, 23, because Paul says
"They that are Christ's have crucified the flesh with
the affections and lusts."

Now the only foe that a sanctified person has to
contend with is the devil. Our sins and our inward foe
(carnality or the flesh) are all gone, but the devil
will be after us until our dying day. The devil works
to hinder God's people by working through unsaved
people, through evil spirits, through demons, through
his imps and directly through himself like in Job's
case. Eph. 6:12, "For we wrestle not against flesh and
blood (i. e., people), but against principalities and
powers, against the rulers of the darkness of this
world, against spiritual wickedness in high places."
With all of this arrayed against us we have one might-
ier on our side. Jesus is stronger than the devil. The
devil is mighty, but Jesus is almighty. "We are more
than conquerors through Him that loved us," Rom.
8:37. "If God be for us, who then can be against
us?" Rom. 8:31. "Ye are of God, little children, and
have overcome them; because greater is he that is in
you, than he that is in the world." 1 John 4:4.

The Christian's job is to let the Lord handle the devil. So many dear people try to reason with the devil until their minds are upset. Learn quickly to defeat the enemy in this, because he can out-reason you. When your peace of mind is disturbed, you may be sure it is the enemy suggesting things to you. "Commit thy way unto the Lord; trust also in him; and he shall bring it to pass." There is a rich promise for us along this line in Isa. 26:3, "Thou wilt keep him in perfect peace whose mind is stayed on Thee; because he trusteth in Thee." These are actual facts, beloved, and they work. Let the Lord fight your battles. Have faith in God and His word. Remember that anxiety is not faith. If testing times come, and they do, just pray and do whatever God tells you to do about it, and then commit it entirely to the Lord for He loves to have us fully trust Him. Luther says,

"And though this world, with devils filled,
   Should threaten to undo us;
We will not fear, for God hath willed
   His truth to triumph through us.
Let goods and kindred go,
This mortal life also:
The body they may kill;
God's truth abideth still,
His kingdom is forever."

A good way to drive the devil away also is to repeat the name of Jesus. The enemy can't stand the name of Jesus.

"Take the name of Jesus ever,
    As a shield from every snare;
If temptations round you gather,
    Breathe that holy name in prayer."

Many, many times in my early Christian life I defeated the devil in this way. "Resist the devil and he will flee from you." Jas. 4:7. "Your adversary the devil, as a roaring lion, walketh about, seeking whom he may devour: whom resist steadfast in the faith." 1 Peter 5:8, 9.

I find many people who have not yet learned to distinguish between the voice of Jesus and the voice of the enemy. David knew the voice of the enemy—Psa. 55:3, 4, "Because of the voice of the enemy—my heart is sore pained, within me." Jesus said, "My sheep know my voice." The voice of the enemy is cruel, nagging, unkind, accusing, driving, and harsh. The voice of Jesus is tender, kind, never accusing or harsh. If you are motivated by a spirit that rushes you into things, it is the enemy. If you love the Word and love souls, yet there is a voice telling you that you are backslidden, you may be sure it is the enemy. If you are truly backslidden, the devil will invariably let you think that you are getting along just fine, and he will let you hide behind that false profession by doing lots of church work and going through the performance of devotions. However, if you are truly backslidden, the Lord will speak to you by putting His finger on the sins of your life and try to tenderly woo you back to Himself. Or if you have not lost the Lord out of your heart, but have grieved Him, then He will show you that too, and you can make it right. It may be you have grieved Him by failing to walk in some new light or by some unkind word or deed. If so, quickly walk in the light and make it right. I heard Brother Bud Robinson tell how he grieved the Lord one time and as he put it, "The little bird stopped singing in my heart." He had spoken sharply to the ticket agent because he was rushing to make a train and had a lot of baggage to check, etc. He said, "I had no peace in my heart until I ran back and asked the man to forgive me." "At once the little bird started singing in my soul." We cannot go on grieving God and expect to keep saved.

Sins are wilful transgressions of God's laws. If we deliberately and wilfully disobey God or break His commandments, of course we are backslidden. Sin brings guilt and condemnation. "The backslider in heart is filled with his own ways." God is very patient and long suffering with us. He does not stand over us with a club. On the other hand, we cannot trifle with God or His dealings with us. God cannot abide in our hearts in Holy Ghost sanctifying power unless we are willing to face the opposition and bear the reproach. Very many, I fear, grieve God here and begin to lose out. Even the sainted John Fletcher of early Methodism in England, listened to Satan who suggested to him, "Don't testify to this experience until you see more fruits of it." He soon began to doubt the witness which God had so truly and richly given to him. In a little while he lost the blessing. The second time he lost this grace, he had listened to the enemy who said, "Thou art a public character. The eyes of all men are upon thee." He hid his Lord's talent and improved it not. From that unprofitable servant shall be taken away even that he hath. Later he became desperate—received the blessing after humbly confessing to his brethren in the ministry in public of his failures, and became one of the most positive exponents of the experience and doctrine of holiness in all of Methodism. His zeal for this truth was unsurpassed by anyone of his age. John Wesley said at his funeral, "I have known many excellent men, holy in heart and life, but an equal to him I have not known. So unblameable a man in every respect, I have not found either in Europe or America. Nor do I expect to find another such on this side of eternity." Robert Southey said of him, "No age or country has ever produced a man of more fervent piety; no church has ever possessed a more apostolic minister." It was holiness of heart and life in his public ministry and private life that brought forth all of these marvelous eulogies of Fletcher. He bore the reproach.

All up and down the land I meet people who once knew the Lord in sanctifying power, but now are powerless, and their ministry is so empty and frail. It puts spiritual fiber into us to live it and preach it and testify to holiness when there is opposition. To testify definitely to the sanctifying power of the Holy Ghost in our hearts helps to make us overcomers. This is what makes our work in the Hills of Kentucky so interesting and our workers grow in grace so fast. Beloved, we major on holiness. 1 Sam. 2:30, "For them that honor me I will honor." On the other hand, Mark 8:38, "Whosoever therefore shall be ashamed of me and my words in this adulterous and sinful generation; of him also shall the Son of Man be ashamed, when He cometh in the glory of His Father with the holy angels."

I'm so thankful that all of our Protestant churches have this glorious Bible doctrine and truth in their discipline and that the Bible teaches it so clearly. Repentance, baptism, and regeneration are mentioned so few times in the Bible compared to Christian perfection, sanctification, cleansing, purity, and holiness. Repentance is mentioned sixty-six times in the New Testament, baptism with reference to water baptism, six times; while holiness is spoken of in the entire Bible fifteen hundred times with reference to a heart experience in a second work of grace. Since the Lord majors on it, why shouldn't we major on it too, so that dear people to whom we minister may know about the wonderful things of full salvation and they too, may enjoy it if they will. Let us not fail to give them all the opportunity they need and then the responsibility has lifted from us. Dr. Paul S. Rees says, "A holiness preacher is one who gets people into the experience." There is always an unusual liberty and blessing attached to a definite holiness ministry. There is no drudgery about it. The rich outpourings of the Holy Ghost are refreshing. I quote here from a letter I received this week from one of our station pastors who is one of our own mountain girls. The letter is dated

March 19, 1942.

"The Lord reigns high in the Heavens to intercede for His kingdom's sake. The enemy has 'puffed and howled' but he is being defeated. Mrs. Swauger has written to you about our 'stonings,' etc. I'll not repeat that, for the latest news is far superior. Sunday night the Lord brought some people to church who had not been coming. Olive preached on the subject of 'Grieving the Holy Spirit.' At the close of the message we were singing, 'The Great Physician,' and a streak of glory hit Mrs. Rose's soul and she was surely under God's power. She took up several minutes in exhorting and shouting. In the meantime some of the rest of us were trying to get the feelings of joy and praise out of our little hearts by crying. After being dismissed, Mrs. Rose went to one of the ladies and began talking to her. She burst forth crying; then I talked a few minutes to her. Finally, she said, 'I do want to go to the altar and pray before I go, and Mr. Thompson, I want you to pray.' And pray he did. She didn't get through, but came to the prayer meeting last night, and prayed so earnestly. She said that she believed the Lord saved her. She had been having nights of insomnia because of her soul condition. No doubt others are being likewise dealt with. The Lord truly answers prayer and we are conscious of God's stately steppings in our midst. The thick demon atmosphere is lifting continually and our souls do nearly burst with praise over the 'mercy drops,' but we're pleading for 'showers.'

"We've been calling some and are grateful for

strength and grace and the burden for souls. Life with all our human handicaps, is worth living when we live only to do the will of God.

"Lots of love from your own child,

"EUNICE."

Sometimes we send letters like the following to each station from the office during the summer campaigns when we have a number of extra workers come to help us. The following is a copy, June 20, 1932:

"Dear Co-Laborers:

"We are sending the following questions to you in order that we may have an up-to-date report of the work. Please send it to the office by July 12th. We pray very much for you and the people at your station.

"1. How many visits have you made?

"2. How many services have you held?

"3. What is the average attendance of your Sunday School?

Of your church services?

"4. How many definite entire holiness messages have you given?

"5. What is your hardest problem?

"6. Are your needs all supplied?

"7. When do you feel is the best time to hold a revival at your station?

'Wherever holiness is preached the whole work of God moves forward.'—John Wesley.

"Please pray for the entire work spiritually and financially.

"Sincerely and prayerfully yours,

"LELA G. MCCONNELL."

It is most refreshing to receive the answer to these reports.

In recent years we have arranged for a course of study. At one of the June Conferences some of the members recommended we should have this study. A committee of three was appointed to plan such a course. Their report which was accepted by the Conference was this:

1. Make an analysis of the book of Malachi and of Romans from a Holiness viewpoint.
2. Study "Heart Purity" and learn two verses un-under each sub-topic.
3. Find ten good, but not so prominent, examples of Holiness in the Bible.
4. Read one biography of some holiness character.
5. Study "Foundations of Doctrines" by Dr. H. E. Jessop.
6. Read Bryce's Book on Pentecost.
7. Read two optional devotional books by: Hill, Keen, Steele, etc.

If possible, read some of Wesley's Sermons, some of Jowett's books, and Carradine's "Revival Incidents."

Now my dear reader, unless you keep refreshing your mind with some definite line of study, the enemy will find a place to get into your life or ministry and thereby weakening your preaching and helpfulness to the people. Dr. C. W. Butler, President of the National Holiness Association and Editor of the *Christian Witness*, (an interdenominational holiness paper) was our conference speaker some years ago. At one of the morning sessions he spoke for three hours with only a short intermission. He fed our hearts on the deep things of God's Word. What a season of refreshing and blessing. These Christmas and June conferences are held at the headquarters for fellowship, rest, and reports. The Lord has been so good to send us seasoned men and women to speak to us at these times. Dr. Butler is our Conference speaker this year also (1942).

Another great help to our converts are the many praise meeetings. We have them at least once a week throughout the entire Association. Rev. 12:11, "And they overcame him by the Blood of the Lamb, and by the word of their testimony." Paul and Barnabas were mightily used of God in testifying. Acts 14:3, "Long time therefore abode they speaking boldly in the Lord which gave testimony unto the word of His grace."

We felt led years ago to have a "Class Meeting" in the Mt. Carmel High School. It has met every Friday for forty-five minutes before supper for fifteen years. Without a doubt it has been the greatest factor of all in helping our high school young men and women to become established in the Lord. The students love the service. The time is given entirely to testimony, with now and then an exhortation from the leader and often someone will raise a song which has been prompted by the Spirit. Let us hear what one of the early fathers of Methodism says about the Class Meeting: "One of the factors for developing spirituality and for using the talents of believers who were not called to the office and work of an elder, was the 'Class Meeting'—a distinctive feature of Methodism. The Class Meetings

were times of spiritual examination, of heart search-
ings, of close application of the truth; and as the original purpose has been adhered to by the leaders, the
church has grown in spirituality and power; as they
have been neglected, the church has fallen into weak-
ness and worldliness."

Visitors who come to see us from all over the nation are touched mightily by the rich and unctious
testimonies of our young people in the schools and the
converts in the pastorates. For instance, in 1940, I
was so pleased to have my sister, Mrs. F. J. Reeser,
Dr. and Mrs. J. H. V. Reese, Mrs. Kenworthy Lord,
Miss Lillian Kennedy, Miss Bessie Helms, Mrs. Frank
Ludwig, and Dr. and Mrs. Wm. Hirlinger of Honey
Brook, Pa., visit us. These dear friends of my childhood days are very near to my heart. Everyone was
touched by the wonderful praise meetings that the
Lord gave us during their stay with us for a week.
They, with many others in my home town, have sup-
ported me all through these years. Psa. 126:8, "He
that goeth forth and weeping, bearing precious seed,
shall doubtless come again with rejoicing, bringing
his sheaves with him." It is in the Honey Brook Methodist Church where I hold my membership. It was
in this same church I found the Lord in January, 1898,
and was assigned to a "Class Meeting."

This church also has sent out another missionary,
Miss Bessie Seldomridge (now Mrs. Karl Paulo) who
came to us in September, 1932. She came to us largely as a result of hearing the definite testimonies of
some of our converts. She is a graduate of the Honey

Brook High School and Pierces' Business College in Philadelphia. She was graduated from our Kentucky Mountain Bible Institute in 1934. Here God called her to spend her life in our work in the Kentucky mountains. Later in our work she met Mr. Karl Paulo, who is also an alumnus of Kentucky Mountain Bible Institute and called here. Both of them went from the work to Asbury College where they were graduated in 1940. In June of that year their beautiful wedding was solemnized in the Mt. Carmel Chapel (we have many such beautiful marriages among our workers).

Mr. and Mrs. Paulo are members of the Mt. Carmel High School faculty. Little Rebekah Martha Paulo, who is named for my own mother, was born August 21, 1941.

We often remind the Lord that we are gladly giving our lives with no salary for the salvation of souls in the mountains, and that He must raise up friends to supply our needs or show us the reason why. If God shows us anything we make it right at once. The wheels of faith must be kept unclogged in order for the Lord to work in revival fires and to carry on the work. For example, one dear friend in Honey Brook who has known me all my life, has sent us several thousands of dollars in answer to prayer. We were in great need one time. We prayed. She sent us $1000. I asked her later about it. She said that the Lord put it upon her very heavily so that she could not sleep. That was our faithful God. The Lord bless and reward her much for her liberal share in the salvation of souls in the Kentucky hills.

Many times I have found the price of leadership is a lonely way. I have praised God over and over again for my early training and the power of stick-to-it-tiveness which I inherited from my mother, and also for the many hard battles of my younger days. "What I do thou knowest not now; but thou shalt know hereafter." John 13:7. "No chastening for the present seemeth to be joyous, but grievous; nevertheless afterwards it yieldeth the peaceable fruit of righteousness unto them which are exercised thereby." Heb. 12:11.

Every Christian worker must recognize the fact that folk still have their humanity to reckon with after they are saved and sanctified. In many cases where people have neglected to get saved after the age of twenty-five or thirty or more, their humanity has become warped through sin in such a way that their battles are harder. It takes great patience, love, and understanding to help them. However, God gives us enough divine and human psychology to vitally help them until they become well established. Mistakes are not sins; they are of the head and not of the heart. Our perfection lies only in loving God with all of our heart, soul, mind, and strength.

The Lord has helped us in the Kentucky Mountain Holiness Association through these eighteen years with our army of workers. When folk are well oiled by the Holy Ghost, things move on smoothly. The Lord has cemented us together in one common purpose. There has never been one split in the work. Neither has one that God has called here for life (fifty-seven in all) ever given the least hint of opposition or pulling apart to the making of a division. We praise God for the marvelous harmony that He has given. Holiness never splits a church—no, it's the lack of it. Carnality is the thing that causes dissension and friction and division.

Sometimes workers have come to us who answered all of our questions on the application blank very satisfactorily. Soon after they came, however, they discovered for themselves that either they never had the blessing of holiness or else had lost it. In such cases, they were kindly dealt with about their lack of power and spiritual life by one of the pastors, faculty members, or myself.

These hungry-hearted folk soon pray through and are such a blessing and stand true and lift for souls. We ask the following questions to those who apply:

1. Do you know the Lord in two definite works of grace as taught by Wesley from the Word?

2. What church are you affiliated with?

3. What Christian service have you done?

4. What are your scholastic qualifications and where did you receive your training?

5. Have you ever at any time in your life been mixed up with the modern Tongues Movement?

6. Are you willing to share with us the responsibilities of the work and trust God to supply your needs?

7. Have you ever been divorced or separated?

A few have come answering the first question in the affirmative when they did not mean to deceive and were not aware of their need. However, in some season of prayer or some outpouring of the Holy Ghost in our midst, they began to feel their empty profession. These, with the exception of four, all through these eighteen years, have sought the Lord and found Him in gracious victory and are now living in Canaan enjoying the good fruit of the land. These four were not asked to leave until we tried to help them over a period of months. One very capable young woman who was a registered nurse, had her A. B. degree and her Bible School diploma, we kept for many months. She sought the Lord often, but evidently was not willing to pay the price. Finally we asked her to leave. She was very reasonable about it all and is our friend today. It's far better for one person to suffer than for an entire group to be weakened. Where one member of the body suffers, the whole body suffers. I have known situations in churches and various organizations where there was one or two carnally minded folk giving a lot of trouble, and the whole body has suffered defeat in that measure; yet no one had the courage to help them or to remove them if they would not be helped. When the early Methodists disciplined their members and their ministry, they were powerful and revival fires burned everywhere.

The Lord has enabled us to hold to a good, clean, wholesome standard so that folk love the work and are supremely happy in it. Here is the story of one of our splendid and capable permanent workers: Years ago she felt that God wanted her in this work. One summer she came to us after she was graduated from Asbury College and helped us in a pastorate. It was after this that she settled down into good salaried jobs back in her home town in teaching and other business. She planned to marry a man who had no call into Christian work. The wedding day was set. God over-ruled. She had a car and plenty of money, but was very miserable and unhappy and far from God. Through the instrumentality of one of our pastors, who is from the same state, and who has been with us doing very efficient soul-saving work for eleven years, she was helped back to God. She then said an eternal yes to God and His whole will for her life. She came at once to us and has been exceedingly happy. She is now well established in holiness and says she finds it a delight to live by faith. She sings in one of our many quartets, leads services, teaches in the high school, and wants to take a pastorate this summer.

Sometimes I fear almost to repeat what men and women so kindly remark about the work after they have been with us for a revival, or for a conference, or for a camp meeting. My soul is melted under the good-ness of God to us. To Him be all the glory. God grant that we shall always so keep walking in the light and paying the price so that God can get more honor to His name continually through this holiness center.

The verse that the Lord especially quickened to my heart for the year 1942 is found in Acts 6:4, "But we will give ourselves continually to prayer and to the ministry of the word." With world events as they are, and so much heart ache on every hand, the Chris-tian and the Christian worker has more to do than ever in the history of the world. It behooves us therefore to ask of God greater things so that the Word will go forth with its marvelous power to give light and bring comfort. It is the Word of God that people need. There isn't much we can say from the pulpit that will lift hearts, but the Word expounded and interpreted through a Holy Ghost anointed ministry will have tremendous weight.

In our Kentucky Mountain Bible Institute we emphasize much expository preaching of the Truth strengthened with Bible illustrations.

Paul says our life is a warfare. In the 6th chapter of Ephesians, verses 1-10, he is giving the Christians some instructions on how to keep true and war a good warfare. He sums it all up in this climactic expression, "Finally, my brethren, be strong in the Lord and in the power of His might." There are wicked spirits who continually oppose faith, love, and holiness either by force or fraud; hence this strong admonition of Paul.

The evil spirit or demon which is most common is that of lust. It is spoken of in its various phases more often than any other kind of sin throughout the entire Bible. The Christian worker meets it on every hand. I feel constrained to speak of but one phase of this sin with the sincere hope and prayer that it will help those who want to be helped. It is that known as "secret sin" or "masturbation," Psa. 90:8, "Thou hast set our iniquities before thee, our secret sins in the light of thy countenance." One of our holiness writers says it is more common in young people, men and women (married or single), than smoking or drinking. Since this is true, why not help the people who through one cause or another have fallen into it, but who are longing for help and deliverance.

I cite two cases here who have come under my own observation, although I could give you scores and scores of them that I have tried to help up and down the nation. A young woman with two years of college work and three years of Bible School work came to us one summer. We placed her with two of our well sanctified mountain girls. She was professing to be saved and sanctified. Through their lives and their preaching she was brought under conviction. They brought her into headquarters where three of us prayed with her. Finally, when no lift came, we asked her in all kindness, if this sin was not her trouble. This is what she told us in great relief, "You are the first ones who ever talked to me about this, and I have longed and prayed for help for twelve years." She said that during her training days she had her mind made up often that she would go to the preceptress and tell her the trouble, but her courage failed her. There are tens of thousands like this dear girl. Let us help them. She said, "This sin has kept me down for fifteen years." She went on to relate that she had backslidden eighteen times over it. She said that this was the happiest day of her life, now that she had confessed her trouble. The devil loves to have folk think that there is no need to confess it to anyone. He knows that most folk will never have the power or the faith to get through themselves and break his demon power; hence he tells them that it is just between them and the Lord, etc. This young woman had been held by the enemy thus for years. When she enlisted the help of others, the devil's power was broken. Never need folk make any public confession of this kind. The result was she truly let the Lord save her and then sanctify her. She was delivered by the grace of God and the power of the Old Rugged Cross. The Holy Ghost in her heart enabled her to be an overcomer. Beloved, this is the sure remedy.

A young man came to us. During the second year of his stay, we were much burdened over his fearful lack of power and blessing. The cause soon came to light. His college and Bible School training made him a very efficient worker, but the spiritual phase of his ministry grieved us much. His precious wife stood by us with her prayers. He was truly forgiven of this common sin, which he said had kept him enslaved for years and which had been the grief of his soul much, causing defeat again and again. After the Lord saved him, he went on seeking for God to cleanse his heart from carnality, which is the seat of all uncleanness. Soon the stake was driven down. The Blood of Jesus sanctified him wholly. We often receive letters from him. Gracious victory is his. 1 John 3:8, "He that committeth sin is of the devil; for the devil sinneth from the beginning. For this purpose the Son of God was manifested, that he might destroy the works of the devil." His confidence in God is sure and thus his ministry effective. 1 John 3:21, 22, "Beloved, if our heart condemn us not, then have we confidence toward God. And whatsoever we ask, we receive of him, be-

cause we keep his commandments, and do those things
that are pleasing in his sight."

Some will say that there is no harm in it. If that
be so, why are such folk always perfectly powerless
and continually begging the Lord to forgive them?
Sin brings guilt and condemnation, and thus the cry
for forgiveness. I will quote a very few of the opinions of medical men and others that I have gathered
from books in the public library. They are as follows:

"The rule is certain that masturbation produces
a number of bad consequences if it is habitually prac-
ticed, and it is particularly injurious in children. Such
children, if they masturbate excessively, progress in
their studies only with difficulty; they are very absent
minded, look sleepy and dreamy, cannot follow atten-
tively the instructions given by their teachers in
school; their perceptive ability and memory have suffered very badly."

"In persons who have indulged in masturbating excessively, and who have carried it on for years, frequently since childhood, there can be observed very
disagreeable disturbances and sometimes even mental
diseases."

"In some cases the habit a boy forms in his early
teens makes him a subject of veneral disease in later
life."

"The habit weakens the nervous system and indi-
rectly affects general health."

"Mental masturbation or "day dreaming" concerning sexual functions is probably more harmful than
mechanical masturbation."

"Men and women of neurotic inheritance, combined with the habit, have suffered nervous collapse during college days. It is scientific to assume that the additional nervous strain produced by masturbation was a contributing factor."

"The sum total of vitality lost to humanity by this practice is great."

If we take the opinions of these men of science. we will have to admit there is much harm in this common practice and therefore it is sinful. Isa. 3:9, "The show of their countenance doth witness against them; and they declare their sin as Sodom, they hide it not. Woe unto their soul! for they have rewarded evil unto themselves."

I was asked to speak to the young women along this line a few years ago in a certain Christian school. I only consented to do so if a number of the faculty members would be present. The Lord used it much to help the young women. I believe firmly that if all of our college young people were given definite light on these things from a medical and Christian standpoint, tragedies would be averted and very much unhappiness entirely avoided all through their lives. One of our teachers of former years traveled with a certain college quartet. In Binghamton, N. Y., they were taken through an institution where there are hundreds of young men and women being cared for because they are ill mentally or physically. One of the boys asked the guide, "Why are these young people here; why this fearful condition?" He said, "These young people are from rich and poor homes, but two-thirds of them are here because of masturbation or 'mother or father fixation.' "

However, I am not wanting to deal with this problem from any other standpoint than that which affects the spiritual life of the individual. In my contact with this sin over the country and in our work, I have yet to find one soul whose spiritual life was any other than a head religion. Purity of heart and life is power. Since the devil never put any sin on anyone that the Lord can't forgive and take away and keep them from it, then why excuse this sin?

The Christian young people in our schools, both the Mt. Carmel High School and the Kentucky Mountain Bible Institute, are full of power and victory because they are living clean. We do not leave them in the dark about any of these problems. The remedy for all sin is the blood of Jesus. All uncleanness is rooted in carnality. When carnality is eradicated, then the inward foe is gone and folk are able to resist temptation and to keep their bodies under and live above sin. 1 Cor. 9:27, "I keep under my body, and bring it into subjection." Normal desires and appetites and emotions are not taken away, but all abnormal, inordinate things are gone. All truly sanctified people are delivered from the pollution of sin. All truly converted people are saved from the guilt of sin and have quit the sin business. It doesn't take holiness to make us live above sin; all saved people are enabled to appropriate grace to keep from sinning. Holiness makes religion easy and gives you quick victory over temptation. "Knowing this, that our old man is crucified with him, that the body of sin might be destroyed. that henceforth we should not serve sin." Rom. 6:6. "Where sin abounded, grace did much more abound." Rom. 5:20. "Because greater is he that is in you, than he that is in the world." 1 John 4:4.

Sometimes the Lord has to give folk up since they prefer these sins. Rom. 1:24, "Wherefore God also gave them up to uncleanness through the lusts of their own hearts." And the fearful consequences are found in Rom. 1:24-27.

Very often when young people become chronic seekers at our camps and in our schools and churches, their trouble is this sin. Often this is the trouble with older people too. Praise God there is deliverance for everyone who really wants to be delivered. I have known scores and scores who have glorious and permanent victory over this fearful sin in all of its forms.

If the habit has gotten a deep hold on folk, their fight, after their hearts are cleansed will be harder. They can by God's grace, and keeping their minds filled with good things, and plenty of wholesome exercise, and will power, keep victory. It won't be long until the devil sees that there is no use tempting them along this line because their will is so set on God's side.

"Yield not to temptation, for yielding is sin,
Each victory will help you, some other to win;
Fight manfully onward, dark passions subdue,
Look ever to Jesus, He'll carry you through."

Just because your heart is purified is no reason why you should not be on your guard. We are to fight the good fight of faith. God expects you to do your part. In other words, it takes will power and control of the thought life with your salvation. We are still free moral agents after the Lord has saved us by His marvelous grace and sanctified us and the Holy Ghost has come in to abide. The same determination that it takes to get salvation must be maintained in order to keep saved. "As ye have therefore received Christ Jesus the Lord, so walk ye in him." Col. 2:6.

CHAPTER IX

Progress And Summary.—Joshua 17:18

"For whosoever will save his life shall lose it; but whosoever shall lose his life for my sake and the gospel's, the same shall save it." Mark 8:35.

The first summer of our station campaign and revivals was in 1925. Mrs. R. L. Swauger and I held meetings which show the following results: Watkins Schoolhouse (Quicksand) 5 seekers; Vancleve, 12 seekers—9 converted, 3 sanctified; Hampton, 23 seekers—8 sanctified.

Since that time revival fires have been burning and the Lord has enabled us to reap a great harvest of souls. Not only in the scheduled revivals, but also folk seek the Lord in the regular services. At Tar Ridge and Happy Top last summer, one of our pastors and his wife had such good victories. I just received two letters this week telling of one soul praying through at Amyx after Brother C. L. Thompson gave the message. (Brother Thompson is one of our wonderful converts. One of our high school boys was holding a Christmas revival in a coal camp up the Kentucky River when the Lord sanctified him). At Lee City, the report came today, March 20, 1942, that two had prayed through and that a man whose wife is such a rich spiritual factor, is seeking the Lord. There were five people at the Consolation station who sought the Lord last Sunday.

While the workers are more concerned about the spiritual life of the Kentucky Mountain Holiness Association than about the machinery, yet it is well organized and carried on systematically. We were incorporated February, 1931. We have an executive committee of five who are chosen from the board of twenty-one trustees. The present board of trustees is: Dr. F. H. Larabee, Dr. Iva D. Vennard, Rev. H. J. Hervey, Dr. Peter Wiseman, Mrs. H. C. Morrison, Dr. C. W. Butler, Dr. Warren C. McIntire, Mr. C. C. Valade, Miss Minnie Evans, Rev. Lela G. McConnell, Rev. Martha L. Archer, Rev. H. L. Henry, Mr. R. L. Swauger, Mrs. R. L. Swauger, Dr. W. E. Harrison, Rev. Howard Paschal, Miss Genelle Day, Rev. L. O. Florence, Mrs. Blanche Haddox, Mrs. Sam Noble, Rev. Lloyd M. Blakely.

We have no paid field agents. The workers themselves and the converts constitute the Kentucky Mountain Holiness Association.

From small beginnings, unrecognized by the world, the Kentucky Mountain Holiness Association has become, under God, known around the world.

We are indebted much to Asbury College through the Mountain Missionary Society for workers and funds. Their faithfulness has never failed. Their prayers have been rewarded many fold. Not only this college, but many other holiness schools and colleges over the nation have contributed their share of workers too. Many organizations and holiness camp meetings have helped us. Yearly, precious groups of people send us truck loads of food. Their investment in this holiness work is constantly laying up for them treasures in Heaven. Through the years folk have sent us books, clothing, furniture, and other things. God bless them each one. We are profoundly grateful to God for everyone who has helped us in any way. God is rewarding them for their prayers and gifts; we cannot do it.

Our work reaches into seven counties through our stations and into fourteen counties through our students. It is God's handiwork. Its history is full of miracles as those who best know its story can bear witness.

The first entry upon our cash book is fifty cents which was given by a little mountain girl. The records continue to show God's unfailing and ever timely faithfulness. That the work has been maintained through these years, is the Lord's doings, and especially through the years of fearful depression and the flood which swept away our entire Bible School buildings, leaving not even a piece of furniture or a dish or one garment. We are founded upon the rock of God's faithfulness.

A few days after I completed the writing of this book, Dr. H. C. Morrison, a mighty man of God and a faithful promoter and warrior in the cause of holiness, went "sweeping through the gates, washed in the Blood of the Lamb." Forty-four of us (students and teachers) attended his funeral which was like a coronation. The Bishop said that he would be missed more than any other man in all Methodism. His vital definite holiness ministry was felt around the world. His

two visits with us made a lasting impression for the
glory of God upon our people in the mountains. He
and Mrs. Morrison have been our friends through
these eighteen years of labor in spreading Scriptural
holiness through these Hills. We praise God that some
of his mantle has fallen upon us as we continue in this
work of faith and labor of love in order to glorify God
and exhalt Jesus and honor the Holy Ghost.

Depending not on past achievements, we press on
to greater victories in the fastness of these Hills.

> "Faith of our Fathers living still,
> We will be true to Thee till death."

We covet more of the faith that subdues kingdoms,
works righteousness, obtains promises, and stops the
mouths of lions and turns to flight the armies of the
aliens.

> "Through many dangers, toils and snares,
> We have already come;
> 'Tis grace hath brought us safe thus far,
> And grace will lead us home.

> "Yes, when this flesh and heart shall fail,
> And mortal life shall cease,
> We shall possess, within the veil,
> A life of joy and peace.

> "When we've been there ten thousand years,
> Bright shining as the sun,
> We've no less days to sing God's praise,
> Than when we first begun."

Acts 20:24, "But none of these things move me, neither count I my life dear unto myself, so that I might finish my course with joy, and the ministry which I have received of the Lord Jesus, to testify to the gospel of the grace of God."

And now, my dear co-laborers, I commend you to God and to the word of His grace which is able to build you up, and to give you an inheritance among all them which are sanctified.

                              Yours for Joshua 17:18.

www.ingramcontent.com/pod-product-compliance
Lightning Source LLC
Chambersburg PA
CBHW031545040426
42452CB00006B/194